The Communist Party of the Soviet Union

A FUNCTIONAL ANALYSIS

Indiana University International Studies

The
Communist Party
of the
Soviet Union

A FUNCTIONAL ANALYSIS

Michael P. Gehlen

Indiana University Press   BLOOMINGTON
LONDON

FOR MY WIFE, WITH MUCH LOVE

Contents

PREFACE   *ix*

1   *Functional Analysis of Political Parties*   3

2   *Political Recruitment*   25

3   *The Role of the C.P.S.U. in Political
     Socialization*   71

4   *The C.P.S.U. and Goal Specification*   98

5   *Goal Attainment*   119

6   *Conclusion*   139

NOTES   151

INDEX   159

PREFACE

This work is offered as a short analysis of the Soviet party system with suggestions for future comparative analysis of different types of party systems. The reader is assumed to be basically familiar with the Soviet system and with recent developments in comparative political theory. The book is experimental in its organization and approach, but is an empirical work in regard to the evidence presented.

The author is grateful to the following persons and institutions for their assistance in the preparation of the manuscript: Ralph Retzlaf and Chalmers Johnson of the University of California, Berkeley; Michael McBride, the author's Research Assistant at Purdue University; William Hill, Research Assistant at the University of California, Berkeley; the Center for Slavic and East European Studies of the University of California, Berkeley, for a research grant and for the use of their facilities; and to numerous specialists in Soviet politics for having read and commented on various sections of the manuscript during its preparation.

M.P.G.

The Communist Party of the Soviet Union

A FUNCTIONAL ANALYSIS

1

Functional Analysis of Political Parties

Can a meaningful comparative analysis of Communist parties in the party-ruled states and parties in non-Communist states be undertaken? Or, to ask the question another way, are the ruling Communist parties of the party-states so distinctive in organization and functions that they can be studied only by contrasting them with parties in non-Communist political systems? Undeniably, most contemporary scholars who have turned their attention to this specific problem have concluded that Communist systems are *sui generis;* hence their parties cannot be meaningfully subjected to comparative analysis with the parties of other systems. Robert Tucker was one of the first to challenge this consensus. Defining a "movement-regime" as a "revolutionary mass-movement regime under single-party auspices," he contended that the political systems of movement-regimes and the parties within them, whether in a Communist or a developing nation, could be usefully compared with non-Communist regimes.[1] Others have done comparisons of different Communist parties and party-state systems,[2] but few have specifically attempted a broad comparative analysis that would encompass various types of political parties.

The purpose of this study is to develop a framework of analysis that can be applied to a variety of party systems, especially those found in the movement-regimes, and to examine in particular how it can be applied to the study of the Communist Party of the Soviet Union (C.P.S.U.) and the Soviet party system in the post-Stalin period. In short, this work is intended to be a first step— a general theoretical framework which takes its empirical supporting evidence from only one party system. This approach undoubtedly leaves much to be desired, but we believe that further systematic theory and comparative analysis awaits the systematic analysis of single units of the world of parties. While such eminent scholars as John Armstrong, Alfred Meyer, and Robert Tucker have published analytic and interpretive works on the whole system of politics in the U.S.S.R., relatively little other than historical or episodic attention has been given to the C.P.S.U. The approach adopted here was taken for two major reasons—to examine the Soviet party system by the method of comparative theory, and to adapt and test the tools and concepts of modern social science by means of a study of the C.P.S.U.

This chapter will examine salient aspects of contemporary comparative theory and set forth the basic concepts that will govern the organization and development of the ensuing analysis of the C.P.S.U. First, we will note briefly some of the concepts elaborated by other authors, principally those of Karl Deutsch in his studies of communications and Gabriel Almond in his studies of structural-functionalism. While to some degree their schemata diverge, the present writer contends that they can and should be synthesized, using the Deutsch model primarily for the analysis of processes and the Almond concepts primarily for the study of forms and role functions. In order to develop a coherent and meaningful model for the study of political parties, it is necessary not only to synthesize but to make certain adaptations. Those will be presented and explained in the following discussion of the conceptual framework that underlies this project.

The socio-political system of the Soviet Union, like all such systems, is one of social control. Control is the purpose manifest in the relationships of the various parts of the system. In the words of Walter Buckley, "it is the process by which, if a man departs from his existing degree of obedience to a norm, other changes result in bringing him back to that degree. . . ."[3] The process of establishing relationships of mutual dependence is a control process. Such relationships, however, are not constant and fixed. Innovations, whether technological or individual, require the on-going system to elaborate its structure in order to incorporate changes into the systematic processes and to adapt the system to the changes wrought by innovation. The Soviet system lends itself readily to an examination of the effects of change on a regime, for technological advances keep its leaders under constant pressure to make adaptations in what were once thought to be permanent features of the system.

Karl Deutsch has argued persuasively that a system in which the controls are adaptive rather than static, can best be understood through feedback theory. The meaning of feedback, according to Detusch, is "a communications network that produces action in response to an input of information, and *includes the results of its own action in the new information by which it modifies its subsequent behavior.*"[4] In a communications system where the feedback is properly designed, "the result will be a series of diminishing mistakes—a dwindling series of under- and overcorrections converging on the goal." Where the feedback is inadequate and corrections are not made, breakdown eventually occurs. By taking into account the effect of friction in inducing change and adaptation, the feedback concept overcomes one of the fundamental criticisms of equilibrium theory, which sometimes emphasizes stability to the point of overlooking the importance of conflict and change.

Deutsch contends that the feedback concept spotlights three fundamental factors: (1) the kind of information needed to lead a society, (2) the types of feedback necessary for system effectiveness, and (3) the levels of purpose made possible by the first two.[5] The kinds of information needed for a "self-directed" or "goal-directed' 'system are information about the sub-units of the system, information from the past, and information from the outside world. Deutsch notes that the types of feedback that utilize these kinds of information include goal-seeking, learning, and self-awareness. It is through this information feedback that changes in the system are recognized, thereby making it possible for the system to adapt to them. The kinds of information acquired and the feedback processes enable the system to realize the following purposes, which are listed in order of the amount of feedback required to attain them: (1) immediate self-satisfaction, (2) self-preservation, (3) preservation of the group, (4) preservation of a process of goal-seeking beyond any one subsystem.[6]

While sufficient data are lacking to examine the Soviet system through all of these facets of feedback theory, enough evidence is available to indicate that information in the Soviet Union is in the process of becoming significantly more accessible, particularly among certain elites, and that this increase in information has coincided with growing self-awareness of various groups. These two developments almost certainly present to members of the political elite a serious problem which might be stated, in Deutsch's terms, as a struggle between the purpose of preservation of the group (the *apparatchiki* [party functionaries] of the C.P.S.U.) and the development of a process of goal-seeking that would at the very least implicitly demand substantial transformation of the C.P.S.U.

In an examination of socio-political systems, consideration of the communications network with its feedback mechanisms is important for at least two fundamental reasons. First, study of the communications network helps to clarify the boundaries of the system. Political scientists with such distinct approaches as Deutsch and Almond concur in this view, although Almond tends to see communications more as a function of the system than as the network of interactions that in themselves constitute the system. Second, the presence within the communications network of both formal and informal processes of feedback encourages the analyst to examine the uses and effects of all communications and discourages him from concentrating only on the highly structured ones. Unfortunately, it is extremely difficult at the present time to make any sophisticated use of these concepts in a study of the Soviet system for want of access to more comprehensive data. Nonetheless, this writer is convinced that Deutsch's approach is a most promising one for longer-range research involving the Soviet system. It can be employed at the present time by using his concepts as the foundation for particular studies and by setting forth hypotheses concerning various roles, norms, and functions of elements of the contemporary Soviet system.

The question then arises as to how the communications networks of systems can best be considered in the study of various polities. What approaches are likely to be most helpful in accomplishing the two tasks of promoting understanding of individual political systems and of permitting a genuine comparison of such systems? Our contention is that functional analysis is at present the most promising approach, given the limited amount of accessible information and the state of development of concepts and of medium- and broad-range hypotheses in the discipline of political science.

Functionalism in the social sciences originated through the influence of the biological sciences. Function came to be regarded as the independent variable in social systems, whose structure presumably was derived from the sequence and interplay of functions. Anthropologists such as Gregory Bateson used the concept of function "to cover the whole play of synchronic cause and effect within the culture, irrespective of any consideration of purpose or adaptation."[7] Bateson also took up the problem of dealing adequately with disruptive processes and sought to incorporate such developments in his concept of "dynamic equilibrium." He thus escaped the failure of many functionalists to allow for dysfunctional or adaptive behavior and institutions, which was quickly recognized by the critics of the method to be a principal chink in its armor. Functionalists were accused, often with considerable justification, of perceiving systems only in terms of the status quo and of giving exaggerated attention to ill-defined concepts of cultural integration.

Max Weber, P. A. Sorokin, and Robert Merton each found critical weaknesses in functionalism. Weber was skeptical of any approach that began with the social whole rather than with particular social units that were more amenable to empirical examination. Sorokin attacked the inclination to use broad terms, such as cultural integration, without reasonably exact definitions. He also was critical of functionalists on philosophic grounds, pointing out as one of their principal weaknesses, "the substitution of teleological explanation for causal dependence."[8] This, Sorokin believed, was engaging in teleological speculation rather than in the development of a more empirical social science. Finally, Merton, who himself may properly be considered a functionalist, cautioned that some standardized functions could be considered dysfunctional, so that it was essential for functionalists to take into consideration "alternative functions," "dysfunction," and "multiple consequence."[9]

In his work *Social Theory and Social Structure*, Merton refers to functions as "observed consequences." He employes the term *functionalism* to include a complex of "significant relationships" and ascribes functions to such phenomena as social roles, social processes, social norms, social structures, devices for social control, and culturally patterned emotions.[10] Talcott Parsons has used the concept of functionalism as the basis for classifying broad patterns in social systems.[11] Neither Merton nor Parsons, however, has been concerned primarily with the political aspects of social systems. It has remained for William Mitchell to adapt their work specifically to examination of the political system. In doing so, Mitchell sets forth four requisite functions performed by the polity:[12] (1) the authoritative specification of system goals, (2) the authoritative mobilization of resources to implement goals, (3) the integration of the system, and (4) the allocation of values and costs. Deutsch contends that this scheme is widely applicable in political science and that it can be used to complement the communications network and feedback concepts.[13]

The first major function in Mitchell's scheme, the authoritative specification of system goals, lends itself naturally to examination of the Soviet system. While the processes and structures employed in high-level goal specification in the U.S.S.R undoubtedly differ significantly from those of traditional democratic systems, the function itself clearly exists. The major contrast with democratic systems is in the greater strength of the controls that emanate from the communications flow and that are pertinent to goal specification. Here, the principal questions should be (1) who is responsible for setting goals at different levels of decision-making in the system and (2) what feedback channels are relevant to those so responsible. The empirical problem, therefore, is chiefly to identify persons and processes of goal specification. The analytic problem is to interpret the information gathered and classified according to these questions.

The second major function of the polity in Mitchell's scheme, the authoritative mobilization of resources to implement goals, is also found in very diverse political cultures, with variations in scope and style of operation. The scope and style, together with the effectiveness of mobilizing resources, are a product of the kind of communications network that is geared to goal attainment. The questions we will be concerned with are who is responsible for the mobilization of resources, and through what means is this responsibility exercised.

The third function noted by Mitchell is the integration of

the system, one with which the Soviet political elite has been persistently concerned. It is closely related to the first two, for it involves the process of legitimizing the functions of goal specification and goal attainment. Integration, then, can be viewed as the process of mutual involvement of society and its political leaders in shaping normative standards and determining objectives. The degree of integration corresponds to the degree of this mutual involvement and is generally indicated by the amount of public acceptance of institutional processes and goals. The effectiveness of integration in a political community is determined by the extent of flexible or multiple flows of communications (as distinct from highly rigid or one-way communications) between political decision-makers and those interested in or affected by their choices.

The fourth and last function given by Mitchell, the allocation of values and costs, is apparently derived from Parsons' discussion of adaptation and pattern maintenance. In a restricted sense it can be compared with the system of rewards and punishments that are related to goal attainment. It is therefore closely associated with the specification and achievement of goals. The concept of allocation of values and costs is distinct from other functions, however, in that it underscores the systematic requirement that change be incorporated within the general patterns previously established. In the process, specific patterns may be altered as adaptations are made.

The foregoing brief review of the functions carried out by the polity provides the background for consideration of political parties in their functional aspects. The immediate problem is to identify those functions that parties perform in the political system. While it would be highly satisfying to avow that all political parties fit into the theoretical framework developed in this book, the author makes no such bold assertion. Nevertheless, the framework should have reasonably broad application and can be utilized in analysis of at least those parties referred to by

Robert Tucker in his treatment of mass-movement regimes. It is our hope that the framework also will be useful in analyzing other types of major parties, such as the Labour and Conservative parties of Great Britain, but that may or may not be justified. The present framework is least likely to apply successfully to the consideration of minor parties, since it was constructed primarily to deal with parties in power. The further a party is from attaining power, the less likely it is to fit into the framework of analysis set forth here.

Several scholars have taken up the question of party functions. Among them Sigmund Neumann, Gabriel Almond, and David Apter have made observations that are most salient to our present subject. In his *Modern Political Parties* Neumann distinguishes between what he classifies as democratic parties and totalitarian parties.[14] He sees the principal functional tasks of democratic parties as "organizing the chaotic public will," "educating the private citizen to political responsibility," "representing the connecting link between government and public opinion," and "the selection of leaders." His comments on totalitarian parties will be discussed later.

Almond and Powell, in their *Comparative Politics: a Developmental Approach*, emphasize political recruitment and political socialization as principal functions of parties.[17] They also note that parties provide a communication channel linking public with political leaders, and perform a goal specification function, explaining that "parties can supply both goals and criteria against which to measure political and economic realities."[16] Despite differences in descriptive terminology, the functions identified by Almond and Powell are quite similar to those identified by Neumann. Political socialization roughly corresponds to (or at least includes) educating the public to political responsibility. Political recruitment is the obvious counterpart of the selection of leaders. Organizing the public will approximates the goal function noted by Almond. Representing the connecting link between government and public is part of the aggregation function Almond and Powell attribute both to parties and to interest groups. The principal difference between the two lists of party functions is that Almond and Powell's is intended as a general statement of party functions while the Neumann list is ostensibly characteristic only of democratic parties.

This disparity between functions of parties in "democratic" and "totalitarian" systems is also assumed in Apter's "Introduction" to the section on political parties in *Comparative Politics: a Reader*.[17] Apter attributes three functions to democratic parties: control over the executive, representation of interests, and recruitment to office. To the parties of totalitarian regimes he attributes two functions: inducing solidarity and direction. Political socialization is therefore an activity of the totalitarian party, but is omitted as a major function of the democratic party. Representation of interests and political recruitment are found in some form in the lists of Neumann and Almond, as is direction or goal specification, which Almond notes without reference to type of party and which Neumann implies is a function of democratic parties in organizing the "chaotic public will." It can be argued that the principal differences among the observations of the three authors result from the effort to fit the examination of parties largely into democratic-totalitarian patterns.

Neumann enumerates as follows his reasons for distinguishing sharply between democratic and totalitarian parties:

> The functions of the dictatorial parties in power, outwardly at least, do not appear to be different from the four features of their democratic counterparts. They, too, have to organize the chaotic public will and integrate the individual into the group; they equally have to represent the connecting link between government and public opinion and, above all, guarantee the selection of leaders. Yet as their concepts of leaders and followers differ diametrically from democratic ideals, the meaning of these functions changes fundamentally. Organization of the chaotic will is fulfilled by a

'monolithic control'; integration of the individual means 'enforcement of conformity'; and, though these tasks are often directed by a 'Ministry of Education and Enlightenment,' the maintenance of communication between state and society is assured by a mere one-way propaganda stream from above. . . . Through such diverse services this leviathan apparatus, which claims at the outset to be the party to end all parties, becomes in fact the key instrument of modern totalitarianism.[18]

Essentially his contention is not that the designated types of parties perform genuinely different functions, but rather, that the scope of the functional tasks of the parties he labels totalitarian and their style of execution differ significantly from the scope and style of parties in democratic polities. Despite his claim that the two types of parties cannot be compared, he has used the same basic functional scheme to describe them.

In his discussion of integration, Neumann again encounters the problem of defining the difference between democratic and totalitarian party systems. Recognizing that "modern parties have steadily enlarged their scope and power within the political community and have consequently changed their own functions and character," he concedes that contemporary parties have increasingly become parties *"of social integration."* Since once more the two classes of parties in his scheme appear to have similar functions, he proceeds to make a distinction between parties of "democratic integration" and parties of "total integration." Clearly, this approach creates an unnecessary problem. The functions of the major parties under examination are in fact very similar. This is not to deny that there are major distinctions in the ways in which functions are performed by different parties; it is simply to say that functionally parties have many similarities. For this reason, the present writer contends that functional theory can be developed and fruitfully applied to the comparative study of political parties. The communications network, especially the feedback aspect of it, can then be empirically examined in order to ascertain how the functions are performed. Through this approach differences in scope of authority and style of performance between parties can be distinguished more clearly, thereby making possible more meaningful comparisons.

Admittedly, the functional approach has been primarily a diagnostic one employed largely as a conceptual framework to describe generalized structural-functional systems. In the sense that functionalism has not been built on the basis of empirical examination, it is not properly considered *theory*, but may be more accurately described as teleological explanation. The possibility exists, however, that once sufficient data have been accumulated from a broad sample of systems, empirical examination of subsystems of the general political system may eventually give more solid foundation to functional analysis. In order to accomplish this, empirical identification and study of the feedback mechanisms must accompany the examination of functions. Otherwise, adaptation and dysfunctional aspects of the system may escape identification and proper consideration. Perhaps most importantly, empirical examination of functional processes and of feedback mechanisms frees functionalism from dependence on teleological explanation and places it more appropriately in the category of a conceptual framework that can itself be shaped according to factual findings and systematic analysis.

Functional Analysis of Political Parties:
A Theoretical Framework

The functional model developed in this study is applied specifically to the C.P.S.U. However, the hope and intention is that the framework can also be usefully employed and elaborated in the organization of data on and the analysis of other parties involved in mass movements, particularly those that have acquired power.

Party functions can be classified into two broad, but interrelated, types. One is the *integration* function and the other is the *goal* function. Political integration embraces any process or activity that enhances the sharing of values and norms or the coordination of effort of the political community. It may therefore be social, economic, or overtly political in its character and impact. The integration function involves both the maintenance of the system and the adaptation of changes into the system. The role of the party system in accomplishing explicitly integrative tasks consists of two primary functions: *political socialization* and *political recruitment*. The role of the party system in fulfilling goal functions, which are implicitly integrative, likewise consists of two primary parts: *goal specification* and *goal attainment*. The four specific functions are interdependent. They are also the tasks performed by parties, whatever their style of operation or the scope of their authority; they integrally link political parties both with the public and with governmental processes. The aggregation of interests, considererd to be a separate and additional function of the polity, is treated here as a primary attribute of the goal specification and political recruitment functions of political parties. The basic framework therefore consists of these four parts:

Integration Functions	*Goal Functions*
Socialization	Goal Specification
Recruitment	Goal Attainment

POLITICAL SOCIALIZATION

Political parties perform an important part of the function of political socialization in modern political systems. Parties in power especially must devote particular attention to the integrative capabilities of the socialization process. They generally operate at two principal levels. First is the level of encouraging general acceptance of the system and of promoting its legitimacy.

Second is the level of encouraging acceptance of specific policy proposals and goals. Also of particular interest to the activists in the political party is winning public acceptance of the party through promotion of its leaders, roles, and program. The single party system perhaps affords the party the opportunity to participate in the socialization process most effectively and authoritatively. Parties in systems with more than one party also participate in the process, but in their case, it is more possible for them to pursue deliberately disintegrative tactics. In either case the party is concerned with integration and the effect of the integrative process of political socialization on its own role in the system.

The concept of political socialization assumes the necessity of teaching and training. The educational methods employed by parties may be either direct and explicit or indirect and implicit. If they are explicit, the teaching process is primarily didactic. This approach is found most frequently in those regimes which have a fairly comprehensive ideological frame of reference. Except perhaps on the general level it is rarely prevalent in those countries most influenced by Western culture and most advanced economically. The implicit approach allows for a more spontaneous sort of political enculturation. This type of socialization depends upon the tendency of citizens to learn about the political system largely through observation and to adapt to it largely through imitation. Strongly traditional or highly consensual polities may be expected to follow this process. Whether the process is explicit or implicit, one of the functions of political socialization is to inculcate norms, attitudes, and ideals. As a consequence, the educational process functions to provide a framework for evaluation and not simply to impart factual information.

Parties are, of course, only one of the agencies involved in political socialization. Families, schools, youth organizations, professional associations, the general communications network, and other agencies are also involved. However, in the party-states and probably in most of the mass-movement regimes, political parties play a critical role in the education of the citizenry. Even in these cases it should be emphasized that socialization is differentially effective. Different families, groups, or classes and individual experiences in general socialize the young to different perspectives on the same phenomena. This can be true not only of citizens in general but also of those who become members or workers in the same political party, even if it is a communist party.

The principal questions suggested by examination of the role of political parties in the processes of political socialization may be stated as follows: What means of communication are available to the party as instruments for teaching party members and the general public? How do these means become operative? Are agencies of political socialization other than parties complementary or competitive? To answer these questions satisfactorily as well as to estimate the effectiveness of socialization efforts demands a level of empirical research for which materials are not always available. Nevertheless, partial efforts can be undertaken as a prelude to later and more thorough investigation.

POLITICAL RECRUITMENT

The function of political recruitment is fundamental to the integrative process, for it profoundly influences the nature of leadership and representation of interests within a political system. It is widely held that parties are instrumental in the political recruitment practices of virtually all modern systems. Assuming this to be the case, the role of the party in the recruitment process may still require additional explanation and elaboration.

At the center of the question of political recruitment is the issue of elites and the circulation of elites. In some systems circulation may be the product of violence and recruitment may be self-recruitment by force or threat of force. Such is often the case in revolutionary regimes or in systems which have no accepted means of transferring leadership. Where political parties have not developed sufficient strength and coherence to play a vital role in this process, military elites have often asserted authority over the circulation procedure, especially at the level of national elites. In highly traditional systems, circulation may be relatively stagnant; elites may come primarily from the families of the class in power or at least from families in prestigious and influential positions. Such elites are commonly socialized with the idea that it is their right and duty to be politically active and to provide leadership.

The process of recruiting individuals from local levels for positions of national political leadership may also have a primarily representative function. Representation may be achieved through elective or co-optive devices or through a combination of the two. Genuine popular elections may be expected to provide a more direct link between the general public and public officials than co-optation. This is due in part to the sense of direct representation commonly fostered by regular elections. Co-optation, on the other hand, may provide a means of more explicit representation of particular interests. In a system where the elective device is widely accepted as the chief means of representation, the aggregation of interests is usually a process that requires a separate classification. In such systems interest aggregation may be a distinct, though related, function. In contrast, in systems where co-optation is the usual means of representation, the role of parties in interest aggregation may be more meaningfully examined as part of the political recruitment function.

Political parties have several reasons for recruiting individuals, whether by co-optive or elective devices. One reason may be ideological. Some systems go through phases during which ideological conformity is enforced by the existing elite of a given party. Ideology may, in fact, complement co-optation as a potentially effective control mechanism. Recruitment may be employed to bring ideologically reliable persons into the political elite. Recruitment may also provide opportunity for advancement that would otherwise be lacking—one that can be used as a means of rewarding individuals or groups or as a means of buying off persons who constitute potential threats to the existing leadership. In some instances recruitment may result from a sense of duty, when both leaders and citizens have been socialized to expect particular roles for particular types of individuals. Yet other reasons for seeking recruits for political positions are to obtain access to knowledge and representation of influential or potentially influential elements of the society and economy. None of these reasons is necessarily exclusive of the others.

Recruitment to gain access to certain kinds of information and because of need for special skills is especially associated with co-optation. Co-optation is common to all bureaucratic structures and is found in highly organized parties of nearly every country as well as in official governmental bodies. Specialization of interests and knowledge have greatly increased the complexities of political decision-making; an enormous increase in the inflow of information and the storage and assimilation of knowledge is now required for making effective decisions. Systems where popular elections have been important instruments of securing broadly based types of representation have felt the impact as well as have those operating from more authoritarian or autocratic principles. The need to utilize this new inflow of data in making practical operational decisions has added a new dimension to older types of co-optation. A major aspect of co-optation has always been to draw leaders of particular groups into the official centers of decision-making, thereby giving them access to the principal party and government leaders and reducing the chances of their developing into an active opposition. But increasingly this device is also used to bring in persons who are not so much group representatives as interpreters of some mass of specialized information that must be assimilated if the most effective decisions are to be made. Co-optation—whether for representation of key groups or for information analysis—is a means of political recruitment that has considerable relevance for the study of political parties, for the parties are principal instruments through which personnel are selected for the decision-making centers of government. Furthermore, parties that are highly structured and that have developed bureaucratic norms quite probably have also developed an internal need to co-opt persons able to enhance the decision-making and administrative capabilities of the party.

The problem of political recruitment may be expressed in three fundamental questions derived from the foregoing discussion. First, what type of circulation of elites exists in the party and in the general political system under examination? Second, how is the circulation of elites legitimized as a process? And third, how is the representative function or the aggregation of interests performed in the recruitment process? In seeking to answer these questions by focusing on the roles of political parties in the recruitment processes, we may hope to achieve greater comprehension of the complexities of communications networks and of political integration.

GOAL SPECIFICATION

One of the principal functions of political parties is the specification of goals. It may even be contended that this function is necessary for the party's existence, for one of a party's basic goals is likely to be its own preservation. It may also be claimed that the only coherent objective of parties is to win or maintain power. However, this is probably a much too limited view. Perpetuating the existence of the party, like maintaining or winning power, imposes certain requirements on members while providing them with certain rewards as well. Among these requirements are that they give direction. Hence, even should preservation of the party be the only goal, some clear concept of how to accomplish that end will still be necessary.

The specification of goals is dependent on the membership of the group. The relations within the group, the group's perception of external forces which affect their own positions and roles, and the aggregation of views and interests from the general polity—all influence the party as an instrument for specifying objectives. The channels of communication through which various interests make their views known and through which those within the party structure communicate with one another are necessary to the fulfillment of the members' function of working out goals. Examination of the relevant communications channels reveals patterns of accessibility and the processes through which accessibility occurs. Examination of the content of the communications enables the observer to ascertain perceptions, important aspects of inter- and intra-group relationships, and, of course, the goals that are chosen.

Goal specification is implicitly a part of the integrative process. When effective, it contributes to the development of political consensus. When ineffective it may be a disintegrative factor that induces or invites public nonacceptance of fundamental values and norms of the system. Whether good or bad, effective or ineffective, goal specification is an element of political articulation that derives in significant measure from the directive role of the political party. The question of what goals are specified must be supplemented by the questions of who sets them, through what process they are arrived at, and how they are articulated to the public. In answering these questions, we may trace the relationship of goal specification to political recruitment, political socialization, and aggregation of interests.

GOAL ATTAINMENT

The role of the political party in the attainment of goals differs according to whether the party is in power, shares power with other parties, or is attempting to acquire power. For the party out of power, the goal attainment function may take the form of organizing for the purpose of winning control of the government. The method by which such organization is undertaken and the means used to attain the goal are interrelated elements that naturally vary from one system to another. For the party in power, goal attainment becomes exceedingly more complex and includes at least two major aspects in addition to the obvious aim of maintaining authority. In the first place, goal attainment has a supervisory objective. This is largely accomplished through the association of party members with strategic governmental bodies. The extent and kind of supervision varies according to the flexibility of lines of communication within the party and between the party and officials in the government. In the second place, goal attainment imposes part of the responsibility for justification and explanation on the party. While governing officials as such may perform this task in part, the party, in concern for its continued effectiveness, commonly takes steps to secure acceptance of its specific policy objectives. This practice links the goal attainment function closely with the political socialization process.

An answer to the question of what goals are to be specified is necessary in order to deal with the problem of goal attainment. Once the goals have been established, the role of the party in attaining them can then be examined. In so doing, a crucial question is how the party is mobilized in order to attain given ends. Mobilization refers to the employment of both personnel and communications as means in the process of securing ends. The relevant questions are what roles do party members and party personnel (functionaries) have in supervising the attainment of objectives, and in what ways is the party used as an instrument for justifying and explaining policy.

All four of these functional roles of the party—political socialization, political recruitment, goal specification, and goal attainment—are interrelated aspects of the tasks undertaken by political parties in mass movement-regimes. It should also be kept in mind that other elements of the polity may participate in the performance of these functional roles. Nevertheless, our particular concern here is with the role of the political party in functional operations as identified by the four concepts.

The underlying operational assumption of the present writer is that the political party in mass movement-regimes, and perhaps in others as well, is fundamentally an integrative instrument. Its own structure, which is built upon an internal communications network, is an important tool in its operation, as are its established communications links with societal elements external to the party proper. The argument here presented is that, given the present level of accessibility of data and of development of theory, this structure can be most meaningfully delineated through examination of the functions performed by the party in the polity.

The Communist Party of the Soviet Union was selected as the primary subject of empirical examination partly because of the author's interests, of course, but more importantly because the C.P.S.U. has not been subjected to the type of analysis that is hopefully developed in the following chapters. Problems of data abound. This book can make no reasonable claim to be the definitive treatment of the Soviet party. However, perhaps some insights previously missed or glossed over will come to light. Perhaps, also, the very classification and analysis in terms of functional concepts can lead to greater understanding of the political processes in the Soviet system than has been provided by ideologically oriented and historical works, valuable as some of them have been.

Karl Deutsch asks in *The Nerves of Government,* "How can autonomy be protected from failure?"[19] This question is especially relevant to the study of the C.P.S.U. It lends urgency to discovering why the C.P.S.U. has been so dominant in the Soviet system and under what circumstances its dominance can be expected to continue. It makes one try to assess the ability of the C.P.S.U. to deal with change, and to discover the means by which it does so. In short, the question leads to analysis of the learning capacity of the society. This is an underlying theme of the analysis of functions and the means through which they are performed. What then is the learning capacity of the C.P.S.U. and how are its learning capabilities or lack thereof reflected in the functional operations of the party?

Political Recruitment

In many respects the contemporary C.P.S.U. is hardly recognizable as the same party that staged the successful revolution of 1917 and presided over the civil war and consolidation of power. Of course, the C.P.S.U. of today shares many of the symbols, much of the rhetoric, and some of the organizational characteristics of the earlier Bolshevik party, but even these have undergone significant transformation under the pressure of maintaining authority over a socio-economic system that has experienced rapid economic development and, consequently, significant social change. By the time of the 23rd Party Congress in 1966, the leadership of the C.P.S.U. found itself in command of an army of nearly 12.5 million party members and confronted with the difficult task of finding suitable balance between continuity and change.

In at least one sense, in the context of the politics of the Soviet Union, the current party leadership is clearly conservative. Whatever policy differences exist among the leaders, they are committed to justifying and maintaining the party's role of leadership in the system. Despite the general commitment to party dominance, however, there appear to be considerable differences within the ranks of the party hierarchy on how domination can best be maintained. The heritage of Soviet values as well as the education and practical experiences of a large percentage of party leaders demand a concentration of social energies behind a drive for rapid economic development. Such development induces or at least supports change that in turn may weaken or undermine the ability of the party to uphold its preponderant position in the system without the party itself changing. Such is the paradoxical situation in which the party leaders find themselves.

That the successes of the system in such areas as science, technology, education, and industrial productivity have imposed serious strains on the party is perhaps most apparent in the recruitment practices that began in the mass party during the Stalin era but did not begin to have important effects on the party elite until the post-Stalin period. During the interval with which we are primarily concerned here, 1956–1966, there was apparently considerable discussion among the party leaders concerning just what the party was, how it could be defined and what its functions properly should be if the system was to continue to make great economic progress. These concerns were reflected in the revision of the party rules and the new Party Program in 1961, the bifurcation of the middle party organs into industrial and agricultural sections in 1962, the reversal of the latter decision in 1964, the further revision of the party rules in 1966, and, through all of these and other changes, the repeated demands that party bureaucrats learn to make productive contributions to society by themselves engaging in some form of industrial, agricultural, or intellectual labor. In the midst of these internal problems the party continued to grow more rapidly than the population. Between the 20th and 23rd Party Congresses the membership climbed 73.8 per cent, from 7,173,521 to 12,471,000. The admission of new members may well have been a device used by the party elite to enhance the standing of the party in the system by making it appear representative of the general population. In any case, the move brought many newer and mostly younger faces into the C.P.S.U. Whether such a development would provide for greater continuity or simply ensure long-term change remained to be seen.

In examining the membership of the C.P.S.U. one is immediately confronted with indications that there are in effect two parties. One is the mass party that houses the more than 12 million members. This is the party that appears most directly in the lives of most Soviet citizens, among whom its members live and work. The other party is the elite of the C.P.S.U. These are the members who serve on the Central Committee; the uppermost among them also serve on the Politboro or the Secretariat. The distinctions between the mass and the elite of the party are numerous, not only in individual influence and collective power, but also in their social and occupational backgrounds.

The members of both groups in the party are carefully selected. Admission into the party itself normally requires a period of candidacy. Many of the applicants for admission take the initiative by soliciting the recommendations of members in good standing, but the party also actively recruits persons of particular skills or backgrounds. This recruitment sometimes assumes massive proportions as, for example, the campaign under Khrushchev to draw a large number of workers into the party. In their anxiety to demonstrate that the C.P.S.U. is a party of leaders, party officials frequently co-opt persons of unusual ability or people who have attained particular renown in their professions. As a consequence, some people such as established scientists or acclaimed athletes may be invited into the party more because party leaders want them than because they are anxious to belong. Entrance into the party elite is usually attained through a combination of being co-opted and the skillful practice of politics. Co-optation is largely based on the demonstrated abilities of the individual and is often related to a person's association with an important functional group, such as the military, the industrial bureaucracy, or the party apparatus. Specialized knowledge, administrative ability, or group leadership may therefore be important in qualifying a person to be co-opted, along with political skills.

Since the party is responsible for providing leadership of the system, the question of membership on both the mass and the elite level is important. Indeed, the function of political recruitment cannot be properly understood without comprehension of the characteristics of party membership. The rest of this chapter is an examination of the general party membership, the party elite, and the character and purpose of political recruitment in the Soviet system.

Characteristics of the General Party Membership

The leaders of the C.P.S.U. have never sought to transform their party into the kind of mass party that is common in many Western states. The party has made no effort to recruit all or even most of the Soviet citizenry into membership. Instead, it has pursued a policy of selective recruitment both by design and by practice. Those accepted into its ranks are expected to be the "vanguard," the leaders of the system on however large or small a scale each individual member is in a position to provide that leadership. As a consequence, the incumbent party membership has sought to replenish and enlarge its ranks by accepting factory workers or *kolkhozniki* (collective farmers) who have demonstrated their capacity for leadership and hard work, scientists and technicians whose skills and knowledge are essential for sustained economic and scientific growth, persons who have demonstrated a potential for administrative leadership, and others in various categories. What they have in common is leadership potential, whether that leadership is to be employed in a factory, a research institute, the state bureaucracy, or another occupational setting. In this sense, then, the C.P.S.U. as a whole is a party of leaders who in a very real way constitute the bulk of the elite of Soviet society.

The period under examination here is the post-Stalin interval, especially the decade following the 20th Party Congress held in 1956. There are several reasons for confining our study to this part of the history of the Soviet party. In the first place, more data on the membership and on the various levels of party organs have been made available since 1955 than for the previous twenty years of the C.P.S.U. This information has been released largely because of the party leadership's concern over the future development of the C.P.S.U. in the Soviet system as well as over its present effectiveness. There has been more critical analysis in the U.S.S.R. of the party's characteristics and functions of late than since the early years of the Bolshevik regime. Not only have standard periodicals such as *Kommunist* and *Partiinaia zhizn'* expressed concern for the party as a viable, continuing political instrument, but since the late 1950's numerous monographs and books have made critical evaluations of all but the highest party organs. Most of these works are sponsored by institutes of Marxism-Leninism, the Division of Social Sciences of the Academy of Sciences, or local research establishments that operate under the aegis of the local party organization. For example, both the Moscow and Leningrad party organizations have set up schools of sociology to examine various social phenomena, including the effectiveness of specific party programs.

Another reason for focusing on the 1956–1966 period is that during the last eighteen years of Stalin's rule, the C.P.S.U. had ceased in many respects to function as a political party. Political recruitment at the higher levels was subject to the intrigues and whims of Stalin and at all levels came under the supervision, and perhaps the outright jurisdiction, of the secret police. At no level were party meetings held regularly. Available evidence indicates that communication flows necessary to the assimilation and evaluation of information, the formation of goals, and the implementation of policy were rigidly controlled by a comparatively few individuals whose basic interests frequently lay as much outside the party as in it. Probably only in the area of political socialization and local control did the party function as an effective political instrument. The task of revitalizing the party and legitimizing its right to rule fell to Stalin's heirs. They have been faced with the difficult necessity of revitalizing and modernizing the C.P.S.U. without relinquishing its authoritative position in the system, a position which it retained by reputation even during Stalin's transformation of it into the instrument of a police state.

The fact that members of the party elite have different concepts of how the party can best sustain its growth and revitalization has engendered political conflict that has sometimes reached the lower levels of the party organization. This was particularly true of Khrushchev's effort to reorganize the middle level of the party apparatus in 1962 and of continuing attempts to compel a larger number of apparatchiki to become specialists in some productive area. The renewed emphasis on party leadership also exacerbated strains between professional bureaucrats and apparatchiki, and the 1966 decision to raise the age limit for admission to the C.P.S.U. suggests that some party professionals feared a conflict of generations. The emphasis on economic growth has increased tension between the more conservative party figures, often members of the party apparatus, and those labeled "practicists and utilitarians," often from the economic bureaucracy and the scientific-technological communities. In addition, the theoreticians of the C.P.S.U. have been kept busy reconciling new institutional and policy developments with older theory and practice. As a consequence of these and other manifestations of controversy, it is especially important to examine the general and elite membership of the C.P.S.U. in order to gain better understanding of internal party politics and of the relationship of the party member to the general social structure.

Beginning in the mid-1950's one shortcoming most acutely sensed by the party leadership was the great distance between the rank-and-file party member and the general population. Since the great purges of the 1930's the party membership had been dominated by the intelligentsia. The percentage of workers and peasants had not kept pace with the percentage of members coming from the administrative and technological segments of the population. Also, the reputation of many well-placed intellectuals for sneering at the party made the apparatchiki seek more stable support elsewhere. One method for making the party into a more effective bridge between the general public and the party membership seemed to be to draw into the party framework more citizens pursuing working class and agricultural careers. Such a course would serve at least two main purposes. In the first place, it would give greater validity to the party's claim to be genuinely representative of Soviet society by placing more party cards in the hands of carefully selected industrial and agricultural workers than ever before. In the second place it would better the party's ability to control the work pace of the productive units of the nation. The latter was probably the primary motivation.

The official statistics published by the party between 1955 and 1966 in *Partiinaia zhizn'* indicate a modest measure of success in the effort to increase the over-all number of workers in the C.P.S.U.[1] Table I lists the percentages of the membership belonging to three principal groups. Caution is required in interpreting these figures, however, for it is possible that part of the increase in the percentage of workers resulted from a reclassification of certain clerical and service employees. On the other hand, there is no reason to doubt that the campaign of the C.P.S.U. under Khrushchev to draw more persons from the work-

TABLE I

Party Membership by Occupational Classification

	1956	1961	1965	1966
Workers	32.0%	34.5%	37.3%	37.8%
Peasants	17.1	17.5	16.5	16.2
Employees	50.9	48.0	46.2	46.0
	100%	100%	100%	100%

ing class into the party had material results. At the same time the effort to increase the number of kolkhozniki was not successful for, despite a small rise in the number of peasant members, the percentage of peasants failed to keep pace.

The general occupational backgrounds of those who made up the growth of party membership between 1956 and 1966 may be examined by considering the backgrounds of those admitted to candidacy during that period, since the overwhelming number of new members came from the ranks of the candidates. Table II

TABLE II

Candidate Members by Occupation

	1956	1960	1965
Workers	30.4%	43.1%	45.3%
Peasants	21.3	21.7	15.1
Employees	46.2	34.3	38.6
Others (mostly students)	2.1	.9	1.0
	100%	100%	100%

provides data on the general class affiliation of candidates. The number of candidates during this period increased from 405,877 in 1956 to 947,726 in January, 1965. About half of the candidates came from Komsomol organizations. In relation to their proportion of the national population, the peasants remained greatly under-represented in the C.P.S.U. The decline in rural population may account for part, though certainly not all, of the failure of the recent effort to increase party membership in rural areas. Employees, a group that closely approximates the intelligentsia in Soviet terminology, continued to provide a larger percentage of candidates than would have been the case if the candidates and members reflected the distribution of the general population.

Partiinaia zhizn' also provides some figures on the kinds of positions held by the working class and peasant candidates. In 1965, the worker candidates were employed as follows: 52.5 per cent in industrial enterprises, 9.9 per cent in construction, 13.0 per cent in transportation and communications, 16.1 per cent on state farms, and 8.5 per cent listed as "other." No similar information was given for working class candidates before 1965. The 1965 breakdown corresponds rather closely to the actual distribution of workers in the system. In Table III, the particular

TABLE III

Work Distribution of Peasant Candidates

	1955	1960	1965
Agronomists and specialists	0.2%	6.7%	6.4%
Mechanics	29.0	32.0	40.1
Livestock workers	26.6	28.7	19.2
Field workers	44.2	32.6	22.4
Production brigades	—	—	2.5
	100%	100%	90.6%

jobs held by peasants admitted to candidacy are noted for the entire ten-year period, with interesting results. No explanation was given for the missing 9.4 per cent in 1965. The perennial difficulty of the C.P.S.U. in attracting politically reliable and industrious peasants into its fold appears to have continued into the 1960's. While Khrushchev's campaign to draw more peasants into the party met with some success between 1955 and 1960, when the number of peasant candidates grew from 47,449 to 99,136, there was a definite slowdown between 1961 and 1965. During this latter period the number increased from 99,603 to 101,553 or only 1.9 per cent, while the total number of new candidates grew from 545,155 to 947,726 or 73.8 per cent. Furthermore, the large increase in the percentage of mechanics may reflect primarily the elimination in 1958 of the Machine Tractor Stations, many of whose employees were then employed by *kolkhozy* (collective farms). The increase in agronomists and specialists was undoubtedly the result of the effort to approach agriculture more scientifically. The decline in the percentage of field workers and livestock workers most clearly demonstrates the party's continuing inability to cultivate political activists among the peasantry. What growth in party membership there has been among the peasants appears to have come largely from the mechanics who operate farm machinery and the agronomists who are on the collectives largely for managerial or supervisory purposes rather than from average peasants who work in the fields or stockyards and on their own private strips. Available evidence suggests, therefore, that the political leadership in the Soviet system has yet to build an effective bridge between the peasant class and the centers of power. Even the abolition of the M.T.S. failed to have any immediate impact on the attempts of the C.P.S.U. to attract more open support for the regime rather than mere acquiescence in it.

The analyses of party membership in *Partiinaia zhizn'* omit data on the professional classification of employees admitted to candidacy except for a single statement regarding the employee candidates of 1955. In that year 53.6 per cent of all employees admitted to candidacy were listed as "specialists." The most significant categories included in this rank are engineers, technicians, and economists. Related statements were made by *Partiinaia zhizn'* that of all new candidates (not employees only) in 1965, 27.7 per cent were specialists and 10.9 per cent were office workers and administrators. However, more detailed attention was given to the sub-classification of all employees who held party membership over the 1956–1965 period. The data on all employees in the C.P.S.U. are presented in Table IV. The decline in the percentage of administrative personnel suggests at least a partial success in reducing the size of state and party bureaucracies since efforts toward this end were seriously applied in 1957. Khrushchev's sometimes vociferous assaults on top-heavy bureaucracy in the government and his criticisms of party officials who spent their time behind desks may be considered statements of policy rather than mere oblique criticism.

TABLE IV
Employees by Job Classification

	1956	1961	1965
Leaders of organizations, administration, state farms, Repair Tractor Stations, etc.	14.1%	10.2%	7.8%
Engineers, technicians, agricultural specialists	20.1	29.2	32.5
Scientists, educators, writers, artists, health officers	18.8	21.5	23.3
Trade, marketing, supply, social service personnel	4.7	4.9	5.8
Control and production officers	13.2	11.9	10.8
Communications & other employees	29.1	22.3	19.8
	100%	100%	100%

Even more significant for the future development of the party is the ten-year trend in the second and third categories of Table IV. The impact of modernization on party membership is rather clearly suggested by the growth of engineers, technicians, economists, and other production-oriented specialists from 20.1 to 32.5 per cent of the employees. Similarly but less dramatically, the percentage of scientists, educators, writers, artists, and health officials increased from 18.8 to 23.3 per cent. Losses were recorded by those in control and investigatory positions as well as by those within the massive Soviet communications industry. These developments assume particular importance when one recognizes that nearly all of the members of the party elite come from the employee class and very few, if indeed any, come from the proletariat or the peasantry in any meaningful sense of those class designations. In other words, the scientific and technical production-oriented strata of Soviet society have been steadily acquiring a larger position and so more political leverage within the party itself. While the data presented here have reference only to the total membership of the party, information presented in the succeeding section of this chapter supports the same view of the leadership of the C.P.S.U. The members of this group have a unique position in Soviet society, marked by their access to the centers of power and their general indispensability to the continued growth of the economy. Their possible influence on the character of the party is discussed subsequently in this chapter and in the conclusion.

Closely related to the employee strata is the educational level of the party membership, for a large majority of those with advanced education are employees. Unfortunately, the data published in *Partiinaia zhizn'* on the educational level of the membership of the C.P.S.U. contain different categories for the 1956–1961 and the 1961–1965 periods, making impossible any direct comparison between the beginning and the end of the decade. Table V contains the information for the first half of the decade and Table VI for the second half. In addition, the report of L. I. Brezhnev to the 23rd Party Congress in 1966 noted the educational attainment of party members through the first quarter of 1966.[2] The data indicate the gradual but steady increase in their educational level. The distinctive feature of this increase is that it has been more rapid for the C.P.S.U. membership than for the general population. In 1965, over 2 million persons or slightly over a third of all persons who had completed a higher education were party members.[3]

TABLE V

Educational Attainment of C.P.S.U. Members and Candidates

Educational Level	January, 1956		July, 1961	
Higher	801,384	11.2%	1,283,548	13.3%
Incomplete higher & middle	1,850,370	25.8	2,852,158	29.6
Specialized	1,199,792	16.8	1,792,689	18.6
Incomplete middle	2,127,862	29.6	2,755,652	28.6
Unaccounted for	1,194,113	16.4	942,693	9.1
	7,173,521	100%	9,626,740	100%

Those unaccounted for probably had attained no more than an elementary formal education.

TABLE VI

Educational Attainment of C.P.S.U. Members and Candidates

Educational Level	1961	1965	1966
Higher	13.7%	15.0%	18.2%
Incomplete higher	2.9	2.6	
Middle	27.2	30.1	30.9
Incomplete middle	28.4	27.9	27.5
Beginning	27.8	24.4	23.4
	100%	100%	100%

Those in the "beginning" category appear to include those in the "specialized" category in Table V.

Specialized education on both the higher and middle levels has been emphasized in the Soviet Union at least since the beginning of the first five-year plan. In 1928, only 1.2 per cent of the C.P.S.U. membership had such a specialized education.[4] At the outbreak of the German invasion of the U.S.S.R. in 1941, 20.5 per cent of the members fell into this category. The purges and the incredibly hurried pace of industrialization created the need for new members in general and for skilled ones in particular. In this respect Stalin was the initiator of a policy of molding a party technocracy to provide the leadership for national economic growth. However, the trend became more pronounced during the post-Stalin period as the party hastened to keep up with changes in society. By 1956, 28.0 per cent of the membership had specialized educations. This proportion grew to 31.8 per cent in 1961 and to 34.6 per cent in 1965. Of the 11,758,168 members and candidates at the beginning of 1965, 4,063,530 had specialized higher and middle educations. An even more significant indication of the trend is that over 1 million, or 52 per cent, of new members and candidates admitted between 1961 and 1965 had such educational backgrounds. All of these could not possibly have come from the employee stratum. One can only conclude that a significant number of persons in the working class and peasantry admitted to membership and candidacy had much higher educational backgrounds than the average member of their class and, consequently, did not represent the typical worker or peasant in the system. ⁓

In addition to the engineer and technical specialists, evidence suggests that the party has sought to recruit persons with advanced degrees, especially in the physical sciences and mathematics. In 1962, about 50,000 members and candidate members were candidates of science. By 1965, the number had grown to 63,120, while an additional 6,783 held doctorates. These figures indicate that an even larger percentage of candidates with scientific backgrounds or advanced degrees had been recruited into the party than of persons who had completed a higher education. A random sample of the dates of admission to party membership of Academicians and Corresponding Members of the National Academy of Sciences indicates that many scientists became party members in their late forties and early fifties—that is, after they had made significant achievements in their respective fields and often after they had become Academicians or Corresponding Members of the Academy. Available evidence, therefore, rather strongly suggests that the party actively recruits persons with scientific and technological backgrounds instead of waiting for them to seek party membership. Such recruitment practices may enable the C.P.S.U. elite to claim with some validity that party members constitute the vanguard of various social and occupational groups in the system, but at the same time such practices may eventually effect a significant transformation of the party itself.

Two final characteristics of the general party membership merit brief comment. These are the age distribution and the sex of the membership. A meaningful age breakdown is available only for 1965 and 1966. Table VII contains the relevant figures on age distribution. Over half the members in 1966 were under forty. They had matured and begun their careers after the great

TABLE VII

Age Distribution of Members and Candidates

Age	January, 1965	March, 1966
25 or under	7.2%	6.2%
26–40	46.8	46.8
41–50	24.8	24.9
Over 50	21.2	22.1
	100%	100%

purges and many of them had matured after World War II. Most of them entered the ranks of the C.P.S.U. during the Khrushchev years, years of political and intellectual ferment in the U.S.S.R. They represent a better educated and more highly specialized generation than the older party generation. In a sense they constitute a real threat to the older generation. The more conservative apparatchiki are particularly suspicious of their career-oriented, advancement-conscious juniors. It was not especially surprising, therefore, that the post-Khrushchev leaders raised the age requirement from eighteen to twenty-three and that the percentage of party members under twenty-five declined from 7.2 to 6.2 per cent in about fifteen months. At best, this sort of tactic can be only a stop-gap, perhaps retarding but hardly preventing, the eventual admission of younger party members. Such a device may exacerbate the sense of alienation between generations and seriously undermine the kind of spontaneous support the party leadership has tried to develop in the post-Stalin period. In the case of the second point, sex, there has been no change in pattern since Stalin's death. The percentage of women in the party has varied less than one per cent while the male contingent of the membership has continued at about 80 per cent. Despite the female majority in the total population of the U.S.S.R., women have been and still are a politically underdeveloped group.

The Party Elite

We turn now to analysis of the identity and characteristics of the party elite in the C.P.S.U. For the purposes of this book, the party elite will be defined as the members and candidate members of the Central Committee. The majority of members of that body appear to have been co-opted because they have acquired elite status in their professional groups. In turn, this high professional status is primarily a reflection of either the position or the combination of positions held by the individual or of the reputation he has attained in his profession. Therefore, the members of the Central Committee are a composite of the elites of principal groups in the Soviet system.

The fundamental assumption underlying this examination of the Central Committee membership is that the co-optation of members into that body is a rational process designed to attain particular ends. The two most basic objectives of this process are first, to facilitate communications between the party's principal decision-makers and the most important groups in the system and second, to integrate group leaders into the party. The means of attaining these ends is to co-opt key figures from such groups as the economic bureaucracy, the military officer corps, and the literary community to serve in higher party organs along with members of the party apparatus. The original intent of this practice undoubtedly was only to share the symbols of authority rather than to share actual power. Nonetheless, once put into effect, the co-optation mechanism developed patterns of its own, bringing Central Committee membership automatically to persons holding certain positions and encouraging the selection of others with certain career associations. The result has been to fill the Central Committee with representatives of key functional groups who bring toward the center of the decision-making processes their different experiences, perceptions, and abilities.

Before examining the backgrounds of the members, we must note the membership carry-over in recent Central Committees. Whereas there were at least two very sharp turnovers on the C.C. during the 1950's, the membership has been relatively stable since the election of the C.C. of 1961. In 1966, 79.4 per cent of the 175 full members from the preceding Central Committee were re-elected, although the size was increased to 195 to allow for the co-optation of additional persons. Only twenty-six living members of the previous Central Committee were not returned. Seventy per cent of the full members had never served as candidates, having been drawn directly into voting status. Twenty-two (12 per cent) had served as candidates in the preceding committee. Seventy-eight per cent were elected in 1956 or later, over half of them in 1961.

The candidate membership changed more greatly in 1966 than the full membership. Here it should be pointed out that data were not available on 40 of the 165 candidates. Of the 125 candidates for whom information was available, 51 were elected in 1966, 54 in 1961, and 6 in 1956. In short, over 84 per cent of the members considered had reached the Central Committee at or after the 20th Party Congress of 1956. Since it is probable that nearly all of those for whom no biographical data were available were newly elected to the C.C. in 1966, the candidate membership proved to be subject to much greater fluctuation than the full membership. Some of the reasons for this are explored in the following section.

BACKGROUNDS OF THE PARTY ELITE

In order to determine some of the principal characteristics of the party elite, the backgrounds of the members of the Central

Committee elected at the 23rd Congress of the C.P.S.U. will be examined in this section. Background information was obtained on 309 of the 360 members and candidates.[5] This included 184 of 195 full members and 125 of the 165 candidate members. In addition, the positions held by members upon their election to the Central Committe were examined for each Central Committee since 1952. The principal background factors noted are age, sex, education, occupation, date of party membership, and party offices occupied.

Consideration of age and sex of the members of the Central Committee reveals that the full members were slightly older than the candidates, but the average age of both groups was between fifty-four and sixty years. Thus, the average C.C. member was about fifteen years older than the average age of the general party membership. Over half (53 per cent) of the latter were forty or under, whereas 86.4 per cent of the C.C. members were forty-six or over. Only 5.5 per cent were under forty-six and only two were born after 1930. Dates of birth were not available for 8.1 per cent of the members. The available figures indicate that, while the party has cultivated a large number of promising young adults, higher positions of party leadership have been largely reserved for older and more experienced persons.

The great majority of Central Committee members were male. Only five full members and five candidates were women (as were two of the candidates for whom biographical data were unavailable). Only 3.2 per cent of the members of the C.C. were women, whereas about 20 per cent of the general party membership were females. Elite status in the C.P.S.U. was clearly reserved primarily for men. The principal means for women to move into elite status appeared to be activity in the apparatus of the Komsomols. All five of the women candidates and two of the full members had such experience. All but one had moved from the Komsomol organization into the party apparatus. Careers in the Komsomol–party organs, therefore, appeared to be an important avenue of upward mobility for aspiring women.

The level of education of the C.C. membership was significantly higher than that of the general party membership. The general party membership in 1966 included 23.4 per cent with only a beginning education, 49.1 per cent with higher or middle educations, and 27.5 per cent with incomplete middle or specialized educations. In contrast, the C.C. full membership included 87.5 per cent who had at least incomplete higher or specialized educations and only 2.2 per cent who had not gone beyond the secondary level. No data were available for 10.3 per cent, so that the latter figure may actually be somewhat higher. The most striking aspect of the educational attainment of the C.C. members was the number who had technical training. Of the full members 120 or 65.2 per cent of the sample had received middle or higher level technical educations. Of the candidates 64 or 51.2 per cent fell into the same category. In contrast to those with technical training, only 17 (9.3 per cent) of the full members and 11 (8.8 per cent) of the candidates had been educated at universities.

In comparison with the types of education acquired by the Central Committee members of 1961, the above figures indicate a slight decline in the number of persons educated at universities and military academies.[6] There was also an increase in the number whose only source of higher education was party schools. In regard to those with technical educations, there was an increase in both number and percentage in the ranks of full members between 1961 and 1966—from 58 to 61 per cent. However, there was a substantial decrease in technical education among the candidates. This number declined from 83 or 53.4 per cent to 64 or 38.8 per cent, while at the same time there was an increase in the number of candidate members. The latter development indicates the strength of the apparatchiki who have exhibited fear of the influence of technocrats, but it also indicates

TABLE VIII*
Learned Occupation

	Full Members	Candidates	Total
Engineering	42.1%	30.3%	37.5%
Science & mathematics	5.6	3.0	4.7
Agronomy	18.5	16.2	17.5
Military	8.3	14.1	10.6
Arts & letters	12.7	16.2	14.0
Other (mostly party training)	12.8	20.2	15.7
	100%	100%	100%

* Tables VIII through XVI are taken from M. P. Gehlen and M. J. Mc-Bride, "The Soviet Central Committee: An Elite Analysis," *The American Political Science Review,* December, 1968, and are reprinted by permission of the editor.

their inability to reduce the ranks of the technically trained in the full membership.

An important aspect of education is the occupation that is learned. The frequency of this variable was also tabulated with the related factor of the occupation practiced by the C.C. members during the early parts of their careers. Table VIII lists the percentages of the membership in the principal categories of learned occupations. The information in this table corresponds fairly closely with the occupations practiced by the members of the C.C. in the early parts of their careers. Table IX provides

TABLE IX
Practiced Occupation

	Full Members	Candidates	Total
Engineering	38.0%	26.7%	33.6%
Science & mathematics	4.9	2.8	4.2
Agronomy	16.6	19.4	17.5
Military	9.2	13.2	10.8
Arts & letters	15.3	16.1	15.6
Other (mostly party work)	16.0	21.8	18.3
	100%	100%	100%

the latter information, indicating the slightly higher percentage of people drawn immediately into party work than were specifically educated for that purpose. This practice probably resulted from the need to fill party posts associated with some productive function (e.g., factory or kolkhoz management) that demanded technical competence.

The principal occupational lines followed during the bulk of their careers suggest that the "learned" occupations of the C.C. members were only selectively significant. Scientists had obvi-

TABLE X

Occupational Status of Full Members

Occupation	Occupational Status before 1953		Occupational Status after 1953	
Party apparatchiki	74	37.2%	101	54.9%
High level bureaucrats				
(heavy industry)	25	13.6	23	12.5
(light industry)	1	.5	1	.5
(agriculture)	5	2.7	10	5.4
Low level bureaucrats				
(heavy industry)	15	8.2	0	0.0
(light industry)	1	.5	0	0.0
(agriculture)	11	6.0	0	0.0
Other bureaucrats*	5	2.7	12	6.5
Indeterminate**	3	1.6	5	2.7
Military officers	15	8.2	14	7.6
Scientists	4	2.2	4	2.2
Writers	3	1.6	3	1.6
Journalists	1	.5	1	.5
Trade union officers	4	2.2	6	3.3
Workers	3	1.6	2	1.1
Others	2	1.1	2	1.1
No data	12	6.5		
	184	100.0%	184	100.0%

* Other bureaucrats include those in the cultural, welfare, planning, and security ministries of the government.
** Indeterminate includes those who spent nearly equal portions of their careers in both party and state work, making it impossible to place them in either category.

ously been trained as scientists, for example, but party workers came from a variety of educational backgrounds. In order to ascertain the career orientations pursued by individuals over a longer period than was indicated in Table IX, occupational status was examined in two parts: first, the career orientation of each member before 1953, and second, the career orientation after 1953. The year 1953 was chosen as the dividing line between Stalinist and post-Stalinist Russia so that any significant variation in career patterns and in means of mobility might be more

TABLE XI
Occupational Status of Candidate Members

Occupation	Occupational Status before 1953		Occupational Status after 1953	
Party apparatchiki	50	40.0%	63	50.4%
High level bureaucrats				
(heavy industry)	9	7.2	14	11.2
(light industry)	4	3.2	5	4.0
(agriculture)	4	3.2	5	4.0
Low level bureaucrats				
(heavy industry)	4	3.2	0	0.0
(light industry)	0	0.0	0	0.0
(agriculture)	4	3.2	1	.8
Other bureaucrats*	3	2.4	7	5.6
Indeterminate**	3	2.4	4	3.2
Military officers	11	8.8	11	8.8
Scientists	3	2.4	3	2.4
Writers	4	3.2	4	3.2
Journalists	3	2.4	2	1.6
Trade union officers	1	.8	4	3.2
Workers	2	1.6	2	1.6
Others	0	0.0	0	0.0
No data	20	16.0		
	125	100.0%	125	100.0%

* Other bureaucrats include those in the cultural, welfare, planning, and security ministries of the government.
** Indeterminate includes those who spent nearly equal portions of their careers in both party and state work, making it impossible to place them in either category.

accurately assessed. Career orientation was determined by the number of years a C.C. member had spent in a particular type of occupation. Table X contains the data collected on the occupational status of full members, while Table XI contains the corresponding information for the candidates.

The most striking difference between the occupational associations of the full members before and after 1953 is the sharp increase in apparatus assignments from 37.2 to 54.9 per cent. This very strongly suggests the importance of ties with the apparatus for upward mobility in the higher levels of the party. Since most of those moving into apparatus posts had devoted most of their careers to economic or cultural activities, it also underscores the emphasis placed on experience in a relatively broad range of economic and cultural areas as one condition for the co-optation of non-professional apparatchiki into important apparatus positions. In other words, about a third of the members of the apparatus in the 1966 Central Committee had built their earlier careers in the economic or cultural bureaucracy or some related unit of Soviet society. In addition, many of those who had been professional apparatchiki from near the outset of their careers had been intensively trained in economic and technological matters in party schools. As a consequence, a substantial proportion of the apparatchiki themselves had acquired some expertise or specialization in one or more areas outside of party administration. The co-optation of such experienced persons into the apparatus indicates an effort on the part of the apparatchiki to enrich their own numbers with highly competent individuals who have succeded in careers outside the apparatus and to secure their loyalty to the predominant role of the apparatus in the system.

The priority given to maintaining the influence of the party apparatus and to the development of heavy industry is indicated by the paucity of formal representation accorded persons in light industry and in intermediate and lower level bureaucratic positions. Since only one full member was associated with light industry both before and after 1953, careers in that sector of the economy can have afforded little opportunity for advancement. On the other hand, it should be noted that a small number of the apparatchiki and of those now in the Council of Ministers have developed special competence in the light industry sector.

The same general pattern is found among the candidate members as among the full members.

A related point of particular importance is the connection between the position occupied by an individual and his co-optation into the Central Committee. Examination of the compositions of the Central Committees elected in 1952, 1956, 1961, and 1966 reveals that at least eighty and possibly one hundred of the full members were chosen because they held particular positions.[6] The figure cannot be more precise, for the size of the Central Committee has tended to increase with each election, thereby making it difficult to ascertain whether the holders of some posts will continue to serve in the C.C. regardless of their personal identities. In addition to the members of the C.P.S.U. Politburo and Secretariat, who are always members of the Central Committee, there are sixty-five or more posts that carry C.C. membership with them. These include all the first secretaries of the union republic parties, thirty-five or more secretaries of certain provincial party organizations (Moscow, Leningrad, Kiev, Stalingrad-Volgograd), and the first secretaries of the Moscow and Leningrad city party organizations. From the government, the chairman of the All-Union Council of Ministers (also a member of the Politburo) and at least two first deputy chairmen of the Council are members, along with the ministers and first deputy ministers of Defense and Foreign Affairs. Besides those, the chairmen of the republic Councils of Ministers of the Russian Socialist Federated Soviet Republic (R.S.F.S.R.), the Ukraine, Belorussia, and probably Georgia and Uzbekistan are Central Committee members. From the mass organizations, the first secretary of the Komsomols and the chairman of the Trade Union Council are members. Although supporting data come from a rather limited time span, it seems likely that the editor of *Pravda,* the president of the Academy of Sciences, and at least one deputy chairman of the Trade Union Council now have automatic membership in the Central Committee. Other members of the Council of Ministers have also regularly been represented on the Central Committe but they have not been associated with any particular ministry.

As yet, candidate membership appears to have no such strong associations with particular positions, although there are some indications of change in this regard. Perhaps as many as twenty-five provincial party first secretarial posts now carry with them candidate membership. Some particular types of specialists may consistently be given candidate status but thus far there is no indication that they are chosen because of particular positions already held. In future, the party leaders may be expected to show more flexibility in the selection of candidates.

The remaining members and candidate members of the Central Committee are not commonly associated with any special position, although the great majority of them also seem to have been selected because of a combination of reputation and position. The co-optation of certain military officers, scientists, literary figures, journalists, economic planners, and managers of industrial and agricultural enterprises round out the list of groups represented on the institution. Some of these may achieve permanent membership. This is a distinct possibility for marshals in command of crucially stationed troops or the admirals of key fleets. It is less likely for less highly institutionalized professional groups, such as writers and scientists.

The association of some positions with C.C. membership is undoubtedly one reason for the relative stability of the full membership in recent years and the lack of this association has contributed to the greater turnover in candidate membership.

The proportion of apparatchiki and bureaucrats among the full members of the C.C. of 1966 does not differ significantly from that found in the C.C. selected at the 22nd Party Congress in 1961. On the other hand, the number of bureaucrats in the candidate membership decreased from 29.1 to 25.6 per cent while the proportion of apparatchiki increased over 3 per cent. Both the apparatchiki and bureaucrats who were full members immediately prior to the 23rd Party Congress were sufficiently entrenched to discourage a serious turnover. The pressure from the conservatives, who apparently were still anxious to prevent a resurgence of Khrushchev-type reformism, was felt more keenly in the candidate membership, where the percentage of bureaucrats and technocrats declined in favor of an increase in the number of apparatchiki.

In addition to their occupations, the status of each Central Committee member in the C.P.S.U. is another important consideration in determining the identity of the party elite. Factors examined here are the date of admission to the C.P.S.U. and the record of service in the central, republic, and regional party organs. Then attention will be focused on the backgrounds of the members who were newly elected at the 23rd Party Congress.

The list of dates of admission to party membership is found in Table XII. Those individuals for whom there were no data were probably admitted fairly recently (at least postwar) and

TABLE XII
Date of Admission to the C.P.S.U.

	Full Members		Candidates	
Pre-1917	5	2.7%	0	0.0%
1918–1937	76	41.3	34	27.2
1938–1945	88	47.8	62	49.6
1946–1952	4	2.2	6	4.8
1953 or after	4	2.2	1	0.8
No data	7	3.8	22	17.6
	184	100%	125	100%

were probably younger than the members for whom information was available. Assuming this to be the case, well over half of the candidates were admitted after the great purges of the 1930's. In contrast, about 45 per cent of the full members attained membership before or during the great purges. Nevertheless, the old Bolsheviks had almost vanished by 1966, only five members of the C.C. having joined the party before the revolution.

Another aspect of party status concerns those who had worked as apparatchiki in the party before being co-opted into the Central Committee. Table XIII and XIV indicate the party status of the C.C. members before 1953 and after that date. Party status here refers to the level of official positions held in the organs of the C.P.S.U. Well over half of both the full members and candidates had no record of regular service in party organs before 1953. In the post-Stalin period this situation was reversed with the reversal being sharpest among the candidates. This information suggests two important possibilities that tend to corroborate the findings on occupational background presented in Tables X and XI. First, co-optation into the apparatchiki was a means of increasing their upward mobility for many members who had already established themselves in other occupational endeavors. This means that a significant portion of the C.C. who would now be classified as apparatchiki would not have been

TABLE XIII

Party Offices Held by Full Members

	Before 1953		After 1953	
Central apparatus	6	3.3%	8	4.4%
Central & republic apparati	1	.5	17	9.2
Republic apparati	13	7.1	16	8.7
Republic & regional apparati	17	9.2	31	16.8
Regional apparati	42	22.8	43	23.4
All three levels	3	1.6	13	7.1
None	102	55.4	56	30.4
	184	100%	184	100%

Table XIV
Party Offices Held by Candidates

	Before 1953		After 1953	
Central apparatus	5	4.0%	11	8.8%
Central & republic apparati	0	0.0	6	4.8
Republic apparati	4	3.2	21	16.8
Republic & regional apparati	6	4.8	17	13.6
Regional apparati	34	27 2	36	28.8
All three levels	0	0.0	3	2.4
None	76	60.8	31	24.8
	125	100%	125	100%

so classified during most of their careers. For the most part, they appear to be specialists who demonstrated their abilities as engineers or administrators and were only later drawn into full-time party work. Second, the turnover in candidate membership in 1966 suggests that some individuals who had been members primarily because of their specialties and who had not become apparatchiki were removed from candidacy in favor of those who had given more regular administrative service to party organs in the past.

Examination of the backgrounds of the newly elected can be expected to shed further light on patterns of continuity or change in the membership of the Central Committee. Consequently, the

Table XV
Educational Backgrounds of New Members

	Full Members	*Candidate Members*
Engineering	10	9
Agronomy	7	4
Science	3	2
Military	2	4
Arts & Letters	2	7
Party schools only	3	4
No data	11	21
	38	51

educational backgrounds and careers of the thirty-eight new full members and the fifty-one new candidates are highlighted in Tables XV and XVI. Of the eighty-nine new members and candidates considered, fifty (56 per cent) had been regularly associated with the party apparatus after 1953. All but eighteen (20 per cent) of them had had at least periodic occupational association with the apparatus. This suggests that the ruling coalition of the party has tried to check the influence of the technocrats and to stabilize, if not to accelerate, the influence of the apparatchiki in the hierarchy of the C.P.S.U. At the same time it should be emphasized that this effort had more effect on the candidate membership than on the full membership.

TABLE XVI
Occupations of New Members

	Full Members		Candidate Members	
	Before 1953	*After* 1953	*Before* 1953	*After* 1953
Apparatchiki	17	23	16	27
High level bureaucrats	6	8	2	10
Low level bureaucrats	5	0	1	1
Military officers	2	2	3	5
Writers	0	0	1	1
Journalists	0	0	2	1
Scientists	3	3	2	2
Trade union officers	0	0	1	4
Indeterminate	0	1	0	0
No data	5	0	23	0
	38	38	51	51

The evidence presented indicates the importance of education to members of the Soviet political elite as an influence both on their beginning careers and on their status in the C.P.S.U. Most of this educational preparation was specialized rather than general, the four largest categories being engineering, agronomy, party, and military in that order. Of our sample, 65 per cent

(120) of the full members and 51 per cent (64) of the candidates had a technical education (excluding military officers and scientists). The career patterns of the members included 54.9 per cent (101) of the full members and 50.4 per cent (63) of the candidates who had primary associations in the party apparatus after 1953. In addition, 24.9 per cent (46) of the full members and 25.6 per cent (32) of the candidates had primary associations with the state bureaucracy (excluding the military). Of those in the bureaucratic category, members attached to the heavy industry segment of the state machinery were clearly predominant, with modest representation of agricultural administrators and specialists, and only token recognition to those associated with light industry.

Despite their considerable experience in the party apparatus after 1953, a clear majority of both full and candidate members held no party posts on the central, republic, or regional levels of the apparatus before 1953. This was true of 55.4 per cent (102) of the full members and 60.2 per cent (74) of the candidates. It was only after 1953—that is, the period during which increasing emphasis was given to co-opting into party leadership persons who had specialized training and experience in some functional service (economics, agronomy, military technology, etc.)—that many of the members were assigned positions, temporary or otherwise, in various levels of the party apparatus. During this period all but 30.4 per cent (56) of the full members and 24.2 per cent (30) of the candidates held official posts in party organs.

MEMBERSHIP OF THE POLITBURO AND SECRETARIAT OF THE CENTRAL COMMITTEE

The most influential members of the party elite, at least in regard to their official positions, are the members of the Politburo and the Secretariat of the Central Committee.[7] The most influential individual since Stalin's consolidation of power has commonly been the head of the Secretariat, who has been designated either the First Secretary or the General Secretary and who also has always been a member of the Politburo. The Secretariat has traditionally been staffed primarily with persons who have been apparatchiki by career while the Politburo has had various ratios of party and bureaucratic officials. During periods of apparatchiki ascendency, several members of the Secretariat have served on the Politburo. During periods of bureaucratic ascendency, no more than two or three persons have served simultaneously in both organs.

From the 20th Party Congress in February 1956 until the anti-party crisis in June 1957 the eleven-member Politburo had eight persons whose primary associations were with the state bureaucracy and only three whose primary associations were with the apparatus. The latter three also served in the Secretariat. After seven of the eight bureaucrats conspired to remove Khrushchev, the composition of the Politburo changed drastically, reversing the ratio of party and state men. For a brief interval, a professional military officer, Marshal Zhukov, served as a full member of that body, the only career officer ever to attain such political prominence in the Soviet system. There appeared to be such acute information problems after the assertion of apparatchik supremacy that Khrushchev was compelled to sacrifice some of the members he had brought into the Politburo and Secretariat after his triumph over the anti-party group. As a consequence, persons with strong bureaucratic ties acquired a measure of parity with the apparatchiki in the Politburo in 1960. The membership was relatively stable until the dismissal of Khrushchev in 1964.

At the time of the 23rd Party Congress in 1966, the Politburo had eleven full members and eight candidates, while the Secretariat had attained its largest size in the post-Stalin period with eleven members. Four members of the Secretariat were also full members of the Politburo. (In 1967, Shelepin was removed from the Secretariat and made Chairman of the Trade Union Council, leaving three members to serve in both bodies.) In addition, two secretaries were candidate members of the Politburo, thereby giving the Politburo a temporary majority on the Secretariat. After Shelepin's departure from the Secretariat, five of ten members served on the Politburo.

Members of the Secretariat, though apparatchiki by position and usually by career, specialize in given areas of the system. The ten-member Secretariat of 1967 included five persons trained as engineers, one chemist, one agronomist, two theoreticians schooled in economics and history, and one with formal advanced training exclusively in party schools and as a Komsomol *aktiv* (one who belongs to the activist stratum of a group, as distinct from merely holding membership). Two of the members, Brezhnev and Ustinov, had developed career specialities in civil-military relations but had done so from different standpoints. Brezhnev had established a reputation in this area as a party apparatus man, whereas Ustinov was formerly associated with the state bureaucracy as Minister of Defense Industry, a member of the Council of Ministers, and Chairman of the Supreme Sovnarkhoz. Suslov and Ponomarev, both of whom could be classified as theorists-ideologues, specialized in theoretical problems and relations of the C.P.S.U. with other Communist parties. Demichev was associated with the Bureau for Chemical and Light Industry, Rudakov with the Bureau for Heavy Industry, Kulakov with the Bureau for Agriculture, and Kirilenko and Kapitonov with domestic party affairs. The Secretariat lacked a legitimate specialist in education and culture, but contained specialists in the primary party and economic fields. Although this degree of specialization in the Secretariat is relatively recent, it almost certainly foreshadows the trend. If so, recruitment into the Secretariat in the future may become more closely related to specific career experiences and training and less dependent on political talent alone. Undoubtedly political skill will continue to be one important requisite.

Recruitment to full membership in the Politburo appeared to be unsystematic during the decade after the 20th Party Congress. While most of the members had concentrated their attention on particular policy or administrative areas, no clear pattern of group association emerged. The Chairman of the Council of Ministers and the General Secretary of the Central Committee were the only two posts that consistently entitled their holders to full membership in the Politburo. The principal theorist in the Secretariat was also accorded Politburo membership, but since it was the same individual for the entire period, it is impossible to trace a pattern in that. Nevertheless, efforts did appear to be under way to establish certain guidelines as a means of stabilizing leadership. The accession of Mikoyan, Brezhnev, and Podgornii to the post of President of the Presidium of the Supreme Soviet suggests an attempt to link that position with the Politburo. Furthermore, a clearer pattern had emerged in the candidate memberships on the Politburo. The first secretaries of certain republic party organizations consistently received at least candidate membership after 1957. These were the first secretaries of the Ukraine, Belorussia, Uzbekistan, and Georgia. More recently the Kazakhstan first secretary was added. If the first secretary became a full member, as did Podgornii and Shelest of the Ukraine, then the Chairman of the Republic Council of Ministers was given candidate membership. In addition, there was a longer tradition of electing the Chairman of the Trade Union Council a candidate member of the Politburo, but in 1967 the post was awarded to Shelepin, who was already a full member. Otherwise membership in the Politburo came from the ranks of the most politically astute members of the Central Committee who had built their careers in the party apparatus, the economic bureaucracy, or a combination of the two.

The Politburo and Secretariat play key roles in the recruitment of individuals to positions in the party, the government, and the mass organizations. A study prepared for the U.S. Senate Committee on Government Operations enumerates the Politburo's staffing responsibilities as follows:

> 1. Establishes basic personnel policies for all elements of the state service (party, government, and quasi-independent "mass" organizations);
> 2. Determines the personnel needs of the state in the aggregate and for key positions in particular;
> 3. Establishes basic criteria for staffing state service positions;
> 4. Develops programs for creating a reservoir of personnel with talent, training and experience in an assortment geared to the present and anticipated needs of the state;
> 5. Monitors the operation of the staffing mechanism with particular attention to the performance of personnel assigned to key trouble spots, strategic operations and high priority programs;
> 6. Selects key administrative and political personnel in the upper echelon of the state service, including the replenishing of its own ranks.[8]

On the upper levels of the party and the state, the Politburo appears to participate in the recruitment of particular individuals. Otherwise, its role in staffing is primarily one of establishing policy guidelines for recruitment. There is unquestionably little if any limitation on the Politburo's official authority to intervene in lower level personnel choices; however, time and the quantity of information effectively restrain any inclination of the Politburo to extend its participation much below the upper echelon.

The Secretariat, on the other hand, has a vast machinery at its disposal for extensive participation in the recruitment process. Most of the policies concerning personnel and recruitment either originate in the Secretariat or are channeled through it. Major changes in staffing policies require Politburo consideration, in which case the Secretariat makes its recommendation to the Politburo. In selecting individuals to fill specific positions, the Secretariat employs a wide array of information gathering and screening procedures. The Party Organs Department, a section of the Secretariat, maintains complete dossiers on all persons in responsible posts and on potential candidates for important positions. In addition, general records are kept on all members of the party.

According to the report of the Committee on Government Operations, a deputy head of the Party Organs Department of a union republic described the department's work thus: "He said that the department handled *all* questions relating to the assignment of personnel in the Party, government, and elsewhere—that even the appointment of functionaries in the other departments of the central staff had to be passed upon by the Party Organs Department. Control over the activities of central, interregional, and republic Party schools which prepared personnel for responsible assignments in the Party, government, and trade unions was a function of the department, as well as the selection of students for those schools. Also, the department maintained the personnel records of the Party."[9]

The lower party organs have the responsibility of enlarging and improving manpower resources. This task is accomplished by identifying promising young people, helping them to gain experience and appropriate training, and recommending them to Republic Party Organs Departments. According to the study of Soviet education prepared by Nicholas DeWitt, the Party Organs Department at both the national and republic levels maintains lists of positions that may be filled only by those having party approval.[10] The party, therefore, is instrumental in singling out most of the young people who will advance in the system and of assuring that many job opportunities go to those who have incurred the favor of party officials.

Little is known about the internal operations of the Politburo and the Secretariat. It is generally assumed that the Politburo has functional committees for major policy areas and that most of the members and candidates specialize in one or two of those areas. In any event, the Politburo is fundamentally a policy-making body responsible for high level deliberation and resolution of policy problems. The functions of the Council of Ministers overlap but apparently do not precisely duplicate many of the functions of the Politburo in non-party areas of policy. The Secretariat's primary responsibility is to administer party affairs and supervise the implementation of party policy.

Far more information is available on the operations of the Central Committee than on either the Politburo or the Secretariat. For that reason attention is focused here on the function of plenums of the Central Committee in order that some conclusions may be drawn about the roles of individuals co-opted into that body and reasons for their co-optation.

The stenographic reports of some of the Central Committee plenums held in the post-Stalin period indicate the communications function served by the sessions themselves as well as by individual members.[11] They also reveal differences in the style of party leadership of Khrushchev and Brezhnev and the resurgence of apparatchiki influence after the dismissal of Khrushchev. Particular attention is here given to the June 1963 plenum that was concerned with party leadership of writers and on a comparison of the 1964 (Khrushchev) and 1965 (Brezhnev) plenums that were concerned with agricultural problems.

The June 1963 plenum illustrates how the Khrushchev leadership used Central Committee sessions as an instrument for enlightening the members on particular problems. Excluding the presiding officers, twenty-nine persons gave formal speeches during the course of the plenum. Twenty of these were regular Central Committee members or candidate members. Nine were non-members of the C.C., although three of these were members of the Central Auditing Commission, which is an adjunct of the C.C. and whose membership frequently sits in on sessions of the more influential body. The non-members included a secretary of the Ukrainian Party Central Committee and two *obkom* (oblast or provincial party committee) secretaries, all three of them apparatchiki. The other six non-members invited to appear before the plenum were specialists: the first secretaries of the Board of the Union of Writers, the Union of Composers, and the R.S.F.S.R. Union of Writers, along with another board member of that organization, a motion picture producer, and a "People's artist." The members of the Central Committee who formally spoke on the problem of artistic freedoms and controls included Khrushchev and Ilyichev, both from the central secretariat, and three candidates to the Politburo, one of whom formerly headed the Uzbek Union of Writers. Other apparatchiki addressing the plenum were another republic first secretary, one krai first secretary (a *krai*, or territory, is a political subdivision of a republic made to recognize a dominant ethnic group therein), three obkom secretaries, Moscow and Leningrad party leaders, the editor of *Pravda*, the first secretary of the Komsomols, and the head of the Chief Political Administration of the Soviet Army and Navy. In addition, the Ministers of Culture and of Higher and Middle Special Education, the president of the Academy of Sciences, the chairman of the State Committee on Cinematography, and the editor of *Izvestiia* spoke on the principal question of controls over artistic and literary expression.

The communications function of the Central Committee plenums is illuminated by examination of this array of speakers. Most of the members who spoke had some special association with the artistic community even though they themselves were often not members of it. For example, the Moscow and Leningrad party leaders spoke because the two cities they represented had come to house large colonies of writers, artists, composers, and sculptors. The editors of the state and party newspapers had to concern themselves with publication of short stories and poetry and especially with the review of literature published elsewhere. The president of the Academy of Sciences was asked to speak probably because of the warm relationship between certain scientists and mathematicians on the one hand and certain writers and artists on the other. This latter fact was strongly attested by the signatures of persons from the scientific community on joint letters to party and state leaders calling for less interference in artistic affairs. Other members of the apparatchiki who spoke appeared to be most concerned with the effect of literature on the problem of political socialization. The presence of the nine non-members of the Central Committee on the agenda of the plenum indicates that the party leadership sought a wider range of information than was available from within the C.C. and that it wanted the full membership to be exposed to that information. Six of the nine were specialists, representing the principal professional organizations of writers and composers and including a motion picture producer and an artist. The over-all session may well be described as deliberation without debate. Twenty-nine persons spoke, different points were made and different views expressed, but almost no opposing sides were firmly taken. Silence sometimes served the purpose of opposition. For example, in his opening address Ilyichev recommended that all of the unions of writers, artists, and composers be consolidated into one, undoubtedly in order to make it more difficult for the reformers to influence or gain control of the professional organization. A few of the subsequent speakers mentioned it (some favorably, some with reservations), but a majority of them simply ignored the recommendation. Toward the end of the session Khrushchev spoke critically of the suggestion and nothing more was said on the topic.

A comparison of the conduct of Central Committee plenums while Khrushchev was First Secretary and after Brezhnev had become General Secretary sheds further light on the procedures of plenary sessions. We will take for our examples the 1964 plenum on agriculture and the 1965 plenum on the same subject. During the 1964 session forty-two persons addressed the gathering on agricultural matters. Khrushchev was the only member of the Politburo or Secretariat to speak and he did so after the forty-one others had spoken. Members of the Politburo and the Secretariat presided in turn over the morning and afternoon sessions. Six of the speakers were members or candidates of the Central Committe. In addition to Khrushchev, the President of the All-Union Academy of Social Sciences, the first secretary of the Komsomols, and the first secretaries of the Estonian party and two agricultural krai made formal addresses. Thirty-six of the speakers were neither members nor candidates of the Central Committee, but were specialists in some phase of agricultural work. They included the Minister of Agriculture and the Ministers of the Production and Distribution of Agricultural Products of the fifteen republics. Ten were directors of institutes, laboratories, or special research projects. The Chairman of the Council of Agricultural Technology and the State Committee on Land Resources also spoke. The others were an agricultural machinery specialist, two directors of state farms, an irrigation specialist, a *technicum* (technical school) director, an Academician, and two agricultural workers in local party organizations.

The content of the speeches indicates that information rather than debate was the principal purpose of the plenum. Most of the speakers were specialists in agricultural administration or research. Very few were apparatchiki, and their positions and the content of their remarks suggest that few were politically oriented. The agricultural crisis of the preceding two years was probably responsible for the choice of subject for the plenum. It served to acquaint the regular members of the Central Committee with the details, complexities, and needs of the agricultural sector of the economy. In this sense, the session was not unlike a committee hearing in the U. S. Congress except for the lack of extensive question-and-answer periods. The most unusual aspect of the plenum was the failure to call upon more of the regular members of the C.C. who were associated with agriculture. Perhaps such members had expressed themselves in previous sessions. It is also possible that Khrushchev deliberately arranged the agenda as an educational session for the regular members. In any event, the plenum was basically a communications device used to convey additional information to the members of the Central Committee.

The 1965 plenum on agriculture contrasted significantly with the 1964 session. For one thing it was only half as long. After Brezhnev convened the meeting, Nikolai Podgornii presided over the whole affair. Thirty speeches were given, only two of them by non-members. The latter were the Chairmen of the Council of Agricultural Technology and the Lenin All-Union Academy of Agricultural Sciences. Among the regular members who spoke were the Chairmen of *Gosplan* (the State Planning Committee), the Minister of Finance, and the Chairman of the Trade Union Council. Otherwise, the meeting was dominated by the apparatchiki. These included fourteen first secretaries of republic party central committees and seven obkom secretaries. The First Deputy Chairman of the R.S.F.S.R. Council of Ministers spoke for that republic. Where the 1964 plenum had the ministers of agriculture present reports on the state of agriculture in their respective republics, the 1965 plenum had the party secretaries do so.

The differences between the two plenums probably may be explained by the differing positions of Khrushchev and Brezhnev at the particular times they were held. Khrushchev had been head of both the party and the government. Given his utilitarian inclinations on many matters, he called upon the persons who were most regularly involved in agricultural problems to discuss the situation in the republics. Brezhnev, on the other hand, was head of the party secretariat but occupied no important government post. Furthermore, he had assumed personal responsibility for a new agricultural program. The persons under his immediate command or influence in the agricultural sector were party officials, not members of the state bureaucracy. Since the General Secretary is responsible for the agenda, it is not surprising that he chose those with whom he had worked most closely. In both plenums great emphasis was placed on overcoming obstacles to improved production, although the 1965 session contained more references to party leadership of the agricultural sector. The general style of both plenums was also similar. Brezhnev interrupted the first secretaries of Kazakhstan and Azerbaidzhan with comments and questions and another member interrupted the speech of the Chairman of the Council of Agricultural Technology with a comment. Khrushchev had not interrupted the presentations of the specialists during the 1964 plenum although he had done so in other plenary meetings.

Certain impressions are created by the stenographic records of the two sessions. One is that the 1964 plenum was more loosely structured and that the emphasis was on technical proficiency and knowledge of agricultural problems. The 1965 session appeared to be more business-like in tone. The Minister of Finance and Chairman of Gosplan were concerned with allocation of resources and the establishment of priorities. The party leaders, who dominated the speech-making, stressed the need to engender greater enthusiasm among agricultural workers and to provide more competent leadership on agricultural enterprises, although they too were concerned with technical proficiency. The first plenum, in one sense, was the voice of the managerial-

technical class while the second was the voice of the apparatchiki who had become specialists. Both, however, can legitimately be classified as information forums.

CONCLUSIONS

The occupational backgrounds of the members and the conduct of the plenums of the Central Committee suggest that
professional associations and specialization are important although not exclusive reasons for co-optation to that body.
Through the device of co-optation the party leadership secures
the representation of key functional groups in the system. The
largest of these groups are the apparatchiki and the economic
bureaucrats. The military officer corps, scientists, writers, cultural bureaucrats, trade union officers, and others are fewer
in number. Whatever their career associations, the C.C. members
appear to be chosen because they are among the elite in their
professions. Specialization is seen to be an even more important
reason for co-optation in light of the fact that over 95 per cent
of the members are in the intelligentsia or employee class according to their occupational backgrounds. The working class is
represented by a few trade union officials and two workers, the
latter probably chosen in recognition of some production record
they set and not because of any significant political influence in
higher party levels. The peasantry as a social group was virtually unrepresented, for every person associated with agriculture
on the C.C. was a manager or a specialist of some sort. The
leader of a specialized group is the one who is in a position to
acquire membership in the Central Committee.

It is through party membership and through representation of
group elites in higher party organs that the C.P.S.U. leadership
has sought to integrate various social and professional popula-
tions with the party and to acquire the specialized voices needed
to make effective operational decisions. Whereas the general

party membership helps to integrate the party with broad social groups by supplying local leadership, the elite party membership helps to integrate important specialized units of the socio-economic structure. On both the general and elite levels, communication is a crucial element of the integrative process. However, there are significant differences. At the elite level there appears to be a meaningful two-way communications flow. The elite specialists serve as inputs into the memory system and as party representatives in their professional associations as well. The party proletarian or the party peasant may be able to serve as a meaningful channel of information on the local level but there is no evidence to indicate that any regular communications flow from his level of operation to the party elite or that they are likely to do so in future. Rather, his role is primarily to provide local leadership and local control. In contrast, the control function of the party elite may vary widely from one group to another in both scope and design. Control for a member of the economic bureaucracy may be, for example, the pragmatic task of fulfilling certain production goals, for the scientist a simple transmitting of information from the Central Committee to directors of research institutes and other scientific establishments, and for the apparatchiki a close supervision of personnel and the conduct of special meetings on ideological and economic problems.

It may be concluded that the party requires dependable access to information in order to govern the principal decision-making processes of the system. This access is provided chiefly through two devices: the recruitment (co-optation) of individuals from the major functional groups of the Soviet system into the higher party organs, and the placement of party members in supervisory positions from local to national levels. It is necessary for the party to incorporate the elites of the aforementioned groups into itself. Also, as noted above, this practice serves as an integrative device by enabling the party to embrace leaders whose principal roles are non-party ones. At the same time, however, the practice also introduces conflict into the party and makes the party the instrument within which policy conflict is effectively resolved. Consequently, not only does the party require the participation of group leaders for information purposes, but group elites must seek access to the party hierarchy in order to participate in the establishment of social and economic priorities and to seek the protection and advancement of their interests.

For many years the party leadership sought to prevent individual members of the elite from becoming associated with particular group interests by periodically transferring leaders to other posts. The increasing demands of specialization have made this practice difficult to continue. The party leadership has more recently attempted to overcome this problem by re-educating the old apparatchiki and training the new ones in technical and complex areas. This apparently has exacerbated conflicts among the apparatchiki even though it undoubtedly has made many party functionaries more competent in their particular assignments.

Recruitment is perhaps the most important determinant of the future of the party. The dilemma in which the leaders find themselves may be explained in large part by the kind of co-optation that has been practiced and by examination of the implications of that practice. Philip Selznick has argued that organizations adopt two principal mechanisms of defense against the surrounding social forces:[12] ideology and co-optation. He suggests that there are two types of co-optation: formal and informal. Informal co-optation involves the actual sharing of power by the old elite with the co-opted persons. While this has occurred in the case of the Central Committee in leadership disputes (e.g., the anti-party crisis of 1957), the actual sharing of power is undoubtedly the exception rather than the rule. The concept of formal co-optation appears to be the better explanation of why persons are co-opted into the Central Committee. This mechanism is used to maintain or increase general acceptance of the party elite as the highest legitimate decision-making authority in the system by establishing definite means of access to key individuals and especially to key groups. This is accomplished by the selection of persons who are part of group elites. Such use of co-optation provides the members of the Politburo-Secretariat with an inflow of information that enables them to make more effective operational decisions. The hope of the apparatchiki is to attain the advantage of increased stability and information without a complementary loss of power.

The sharing of the symbols of authority, however, opens the door to pressure for a transfer of real power to the co-opted parties. To prevent this development requires some form of control (Selznick contends informal control) over the co-opted elements. These forces—the sharing of symbols of authority and the placement of controls over those with whom authority is seemingly shared—create tension between representation and participation on the one hand and integration and regulation on the other. Such tension is suggested by the addition of apparatus-associated persons to the Central Committee in 1966 (especially among the candidates) and the corresponding decrease in the more diffuse technocratic contingent. The relative stability of the full membership, however, indicates that certain groups and individuals had acquired representation by right and and that only a major conflict would overturn the general balance of forces. Candidacy may be a means of giving ostensible authority and recognition to those less firmly entrenched but ambitious to secure recognition for themselves and their professional associates.

Reasons for the conflict and additional problems of maintaining stability are discussed in the chapters on goal specification and goal attainment. The roles of the general party membership in party operations are examined in the chapters on political socialization and goal attainment. After these matters are dealt with, we can return to a more comprehensive evaluation of the structural-functional problems of the C.P.S.U.

3

The Role of the C.P.S.U. in Political Socialization

Political socialization, like political recruitment, is essentially an integrative process that the C.P.S.U employs to unify the populace in support of the system and the party's role in the system. Whereas political recruitment serves to integrate elites from functional groups and to provide leadership at all levels in the system, political socialization is primarily a teaching or training function by which the party organization persuades the general public of the legitimacy and correctness of the system and of the goals articulated by the system's leadership. In both of these functions the C.P.S.U. plays a vital and predominant role.

The objectives of the C.P.S.U. leadership in designing the formal means and goals of political socialization are, from the party's standpoint, similar to those of other political parties in other systems. They include encouraging the people to accept the general system and specific systemic goals defined by the party leadership. Included in the former is the persistent aim of winning acceptance of the C.P.S.U., through promoting its program, its roles in the system, and its leaders. The distinguishing characteristics of the C.P.S.U. when compared with non-Communist parties are its exclusive role as the only party in the system and the scope of its interests and authority in carrying

out its political socialization function. Indeed, the party's traditional approach to this function has been marked by reluctance to
accept, and often by hostility towards, informal and spontaneous
forms of political socialization. This attitude is clearly manifested
in party propaganda on the "new Soviet man," the model Soviet
citizen profoundly imbued with socialist patriotism, desire to
advance the affairs of Communism, high humanism, "comradely and brotherly" relations with others, collectivism and
comradely interdependence, and the desire to promote the
further education and development of the people.[1]

Partly as a result of ideological factors and partly as a result
of the party leaders' historic reluctance to rely on a loosely
structured socialization process, the C.P.S.U. continues to em-
ploy a highly didactic teaching method in its effort to inculcate
particular standards and values. The party's teaching concern
is catholic in scope but two basic aspects of the party's conscious
plan of political socialization can be differentiated. The first is
ideological and includes teaching the basic Marxist-Leninist
theories that justify the Soviet system, stating the principal immediate policy objectives of the regime, and promoting certain
standards as guidelines in individual and group relationships.
The second aspect is one commonly designated by Soviet writers
as the "practical." By this is meant productive leadership in economic development. This area of didactic training is increasingly
referred to in Soviet parlance as "ideological," thus associating
it with the inculcation of explicit values. One recent Soviet work
asserts, "The unity of ideological and organizational activity
is a principle of party leadership," and goes on to stress the relationship of organizational work and ideological education to
production.[2]

In both the ideological and the practical aspects of the party's
political socialization efforts, there have been indications in the
post-Stalin period of a desire to develop a more imaginative approach than before toward political education. Much of this

concern is apparently related to the growing complexities of urban and industrial life and to the lack of seriousness with which some (how many cannot be ascertained) young people, especially university students, seem to approach ideological issues. In addition, the diminution of terror has led the party to rely more on the political socialization processes as means of legitimizing the system. These factors, especially in light of social and economic changes taking place in the U.S.S.R. have caused some party leaders to show renewed concern with the ideological and related education programs of the C.P.S.U.

The way that the Soviet system blends value indoctrination and practical education is particularly apparent in recent works published by party schools and by the Social Science Division of the Academy of Sciences. *Voprosy partiinogo stroitel'stva*, released by the Leningrad Higher Party School in 1965 for the guidance of party workers, is especially revealing of concern for this problem. *Ideologicheskaia rabota partiinykh organizatsii*, published jointly by the Higher Party School of Moscow and the Social Science Division of the Academy of Sciences in 1963, also contains much useful information.

Ideological work, according to the Leningrad publication, should be directed toward establishing the concrete conditions for the building of Communism. In order to meet this objective, ideological workers must focus on certain problems:

Creation of the material technical base of Communism

Socialist production relations

Further widening of socialist democracy and the gradual transferal of the socialist government to social, Communist self-government

Rapid development of Soviet science, technology, and culture

Struggle against bourgeois ideology

Following principles of Marxism-Leninism against dogmatism and revisionism.[3]

The very order of the items indicates a set of priorities. Production-related propaganda that may have practical consequences is emphasized over the philosophical aspects of ideology. A major objective of this type of ideological work is to develop an achievement orientation in which the practical consequence takes precedence over the theoretical design.

A similar appraisal of ideological work is found in *Ideologicheskaia rabota partiinykh organizatsii.* First, the authors emphasize building the material-technical base of Communism. Acknowledging the existence of group interests and conflict over budgetary and resource allocations, they add that the achievement of this aim is "unthinkable without the maximal harmony of all parts and sections of socialist economy."[4] Second, they describe the gradual transformation of the socialist state into a Communist society of self-government. This means that "in time the methods of regulating the life of society will become persuasion, the education of the masses." Third, they say that the activity of the party must include "the most important purpose of ideological work," namely the carrying out of decisions "of the party congresses, C.C. plenums, documents of the C.C., the party's development of Marxist-Leninist theory to the broad masses and soliciting their creative activity in constructing Communism." Fourth, ideological work should help create "the new man with Communist character, habits and morality."[5] Fifth and last, ideological work also must include informing the masses of international relations, peaceful co-existence, and the struggle against bourgeois ideology.

The emphasis on the relation of ideological work to economic development is apparent in both studies. The principal distinctions between them is that the 1965 work explicitly stresses how important are science and technology to the fulfillment of economic objectives, and the 1963 publication devotes more attention to the need for the political education of the populace and the molding of the new Soviet man in the values and behavior patterns laid down by the party leadership. Both works assume a threat from bourgeois ideology, an attitude which may partially reflect the traditional Soviet stereotype of the West as continually working to undermine loyalty of citizens, but which also may be based partly on a realistic assessment of popular expectations and ambitions that owe more to economic and social changes in the system than to indoctrination programs. Despite these differences, both works accept the proposition that ideological work should be primarily directed toward concrete ends related to economic and cultural advancement. Abstract Marxist-Leninist theory provides the general framework and part of the vocabulary, but the recent thrust of ideological work is toward the specific and the productive.

The activities of ideological workers in the system generally may be classed as either propaganda or agitation. From the *Agitprop* section of the Central Committee of the C.P.S.U. to the primary party organizations, the party has an army of workers trained in a combative style of political education. Originally propaganda referred to impersonal mass techniques of political training, especially through the use of the press. Agitation was more personal in nature, usually requiring the agitator to be present at various forms of meetings, demonstrations, reports, and other forums of personal communication. In recent years the distinction between the two has sometimes been blurred by Soviet writers so that the terms may become interchangeable. In any event, propaganda and agitation have a common aim—"to instill in every person high moral principles, namely in the moral code of the building of Communism and every possible advancement of the political and labor activities of the workers."[6]

The training of cadres as propagandists or agitators assumes particular importance in view of the emphasis on explicit forms of political socialization. The political education of these cadres begins in political schools that teach elementary economic and political knowledge.[7] Next, they study the history of the C.P.S.U., political economics, and philosophy in schools of Marxism-Leninism. After the cadre member begins his activities as propagandist or agitator or enters part-time employment in some other capacity, independent forms of education are available, especially for those who teach in universities of Marxism-Leninism, schools of party-economic activists, or philosophical seminars. In the Leningrad province about 30 per cent of all political education is independent. As a further step, universities of Marxism-Leninism are available for those singled out as most promising. These universities also conduct special courses for the city and provincial party organizations. Finally, propagandists in the obkoms, *kraikoms* (territorial party committees), and republic central committees are assigned to take courses in the Academy of Social Sciences and the Higher Party School of the C.P.S.U. Central Committee.[8]

An important means of synchronizing the methods and emphases of propagandists and agitators are the periodic national meetings of the supervisors of political education affairs. These meetings are in effect short-term courses convened either by the Agit-Prop Section of the Central Committee or jointly by the republic party departments of agitation and propaganda. These courses are held for the secretaries of province and city party committees in charge of ideological questions (usually the third secretaries of obkoms and *gorkoms* (city party committees), for the direction of the propaganda and agitation departments of union-republic party central committees and province committees of the party, and for editors of republic, territory and province newspapers.[9]

The courses include lectures on the highlights of the most recent party congress and on the problems of industry, agriculture, and foreign affairs. Lectures and reports are delivered by officials of the central party apparatus, by union and republic ministers, by representatives from Gosplan, the State Economic

Commission, and the State Commission for New Technology. In addition, Academicians and Corresponding members of the Academy of Sciences, the V. I. Lenin All-Union Academy of Agriculture, and officials of the Institute of Marxism-Leninism discuss either practical economic questions or problems in the theory and practice of building Communism. The contents of the courses are therefore closely related to current policy problems and goal objectives.

The officials attending the high-level courses on propaganda must then take the message to the smaller geographic domains for which they are responsible. Under the supervision of the obkoms, the city, area, and primary party committees conduct programs for propagandists similar to the ones held nationally. For example, in the Leningrad oblast, propagandists assemble monthly in a seminar to hear lectures from specialists on economic and political problems and on theoretical questions of Marxism-Leninism.[10] *Ideologicheskaia rabota partiinykh organizatsii* reported that the Moscow gorkom, *raikoms* (district party committees), and primary party organizations advanced the education of propaganda cadres through seminars and theoretical and methodological conferences conducted by specialists on propaganda, schools of masters of propaganda, excursions, and meetings.[11] Party, Soviet, economic workers, innovators in production, and leaders of "collective Communist work" addressed the propagandists. The report concluded that "by these means the propagandists were constantly presented with concrete problems."

It is clear from the context of both the national and regional meetings that economic productivity was more strongly emphasized than were strictly theoretical matters. What is important but not clear from the available evidence is the strength and effectiveness of the propaganda schools outside the principal provinces and cities. Methods that are successful in Moscow and Leningrad may not be so effective in rural regions or in areas where most of the populace are one of the national minorities.

Concern of high party officials about the effectiveness of agit-prop activities in the post-Stalin period was shown by the founding in 1956 of *Agitator,* a journal for party cadres engaged in agitation, and by the publication elsewhere of criticism of some techniques commonly used by agitators. Both in regard to the journal and the critical comment, a chief question was that of practical versus theoretical ideological work. *Pravda,* in announcing the new publication, declared that "it will illuminate major questions of the domestic and foreign policy of the Communist Party and the Soviet government, generalize the positive experience of mass political work and the organization of socialist competition, and popularize advanced experience and production in industry and agriculture."[12] Criticism includes that levied against "those agitators who are concerned only with the formal presentation of a world outlook rather than with demonstrating how this world view relates to the correction of defective production."[13] The same source warned against "conservatism in political education" and asserted that new methods should be tried.[14] The Central Committee declared that party organs should be given latitude to develop new forms and means of ideological work, with the primary aim of increasing the unity of the party leadership with the masses.[15] The same point was made by literary means, as when *Izvestiia* for July 3, 1966, published a short story entitled "The Propagandist" that explained how one should emphasize the practical in propaganda work as a means of enhancing the effect of current economic reform measures.

On March 11, 1959, the Central Committee released a statement which said that it "considers the recruitment, distribution, and education of agitators important problems." In order to alleviate the scarcity of agitators, the Central Committee recommended (1) the promotion of agitators from the ranks of well-prepared Communists, Komsomol members, production workers, and intelligentsia; (2) the regular use of means to inform agitators on important questions of domestic and foreign policy; (3) the regular use of seminars for agitators on methods of mass agitation; and (4) provision to assure that well-prepared Communists from the ranks of the *aktiv* rather than only party secretaries are engaged in agitation.[16] *Pravda* for October 1, 1964, reemphasized the same concern for propagandists. In an editorial on the beginning of the new school year, it noted: "The Party committees must pay attention first and foremost to the propagandists. The ideological level of the lessons depends first of all on propaganda cadres. They should be politically and theoretically mature, confirmed, passionate fighters for Communism, masters of the art of propaganda, and must talk frankly and sincerely with the working people."

In addition to the professional propagandists and agitators, each individual party member, especially when acting through the primary party organization, is expected to engage in political education. Three or more members of a primary organization may organize a party group to promote "party influence . . . in the struggle for successes in production."[17] The primary party organizations themselves are deemed to have a crucial role in the effort to unite the party with the masses. "They stand closest of all to the masses, are created in plants and factories, on collective and state farms, in administrative and educational establishments—here where the Soviet people work, where the policies of the party are immediately realized."[18] It is from the primary organizations and party groups that agitators are sent to work in shops, brigades, departments, and elsewhere to spur non-party people to make every effort to fulfill party policies.

To unite the efforts of non-party with those of party members is a primary objective. Indeed, "political work with the masses is the most important responsibility of the primary party organization," according to a principal Soviet source.[19] The party member, operating through the local unit of the party, is expected to cultivate non-party activists. "From the non-party emerge people who are very near the party and who in effect stand in its ranks."[20] Party activists are therefore responsible for helping to cultivate new activists outside the party; they are part of a screening process that identifies reliable local leaders and selects new members for the party.

PROPAGANDA AND AGITATION IN LENINGRAD

Leningrad may not offer the most typical examples of agit-prop activities and techniques, for the party organization in that city is reputed to be one of the most conservative in the C.P.S.U. Nevertheless, *Voprosy partiinogo stroitel'stva* provides more recent information on the Leningrad party organization than is available for any other subdivision of the party. We will therefore take the Leningrad obkom as an instance of political education at the provincial and local level, and supplement our examination of it with other evidence derived from party units in Moscow and elsewhere.

The *obkom* (oblast committee of the party) of the Leningrad oblast has principal responsibility for overseeing the political education work of the city and *raion* (district) party organizations. The third secretary of the obkom is responsible for ideological and political education affairs. The third secretary of the Leningrad gorkom works closely with him. On the next subordinate level are the raion party committees (*raikom*) where again the third secretary ordinarily holds corresponding responsibilities. In addition to the third secretaries, the obkom, gorkom, and raikoms each have a Department of Propaganda and Agitation with sections for the press, schools, and scientific establishments, and sometimes for other groups as well.[21] Below the raikoms are the primary party organizations, only the larger of which are likely to have full-time agit-prop specialists in their executive committees. It is clear from the regional meetings of propagandists and agitators mentioned previously that there are regular communication channels among the secretaries and, while there is not much supporting evidence, there apparently is also departmental coordination at least between the obkom and raikom departments if not among the departments on the raikom level.

Training, reeducation, and special reports for the use of agit-prop specialists are provided by the Leningrad University of Marxism-Leninism and by the Leningrad obkom's Institute of Social Science Research, as well as by the central party organs. It has been claimed that seven thousand specialists study "regularly," but not necessarily full time at the University of Marxism-Leninism in Leningrad.[22] The course work appears to be patterned on that of the Higher Party School and stresses such subjects as the history of the C.P.S.U., philosophy of Marxism-Leninism, political economy, and practical economies. It is reported that in general, the system of education in the Leningrad party organization has four major areas, paralleling the course division at the University of Marxism-Leninism: (1) history of party development, (2) philosophical disciplines, (3) economic studies (political economy and practical economics), and (4) questions of current politics.[23] The latter is not an independent study at the university and apparently is included by the party as a means of reinforcing the line taken by mass communications on current policies.

The Social Science Institute is one of the available training grounds for activities in political education. More importantly, its research staff studies problems of agitation and propaganda and investigates the effectiveness of techniques employed. Sections of the institute examine such topics as the tempo of scientific-technical progress in the present period of Communist construction (as distinct from socialist construction) in the U.S.S.R.; the preparation and utilization of young engineers in industry, research, and project organization; changes in the cost and character of work resulting from technical progress; the formation of a Communist attitude toward work by young workers; the participation of society in the education of the rising generation; the development of forms of social control; television as a means of ideological-political education of workers; the formation of moral ideals of young workers; and forms of leisure and their influence on moral attitudes.[24] This list of research topics is most illuminating, for it strongly suggests that Soviet social scientists are moving toward a more empirical form of investigation and that the party (or more precisely in this instance, the Leningrad obkom) is supporting that move. The reasons are clear. The party leadership wants to measure the effectiveness of its work and it cannot do so with dogmatic and non-empirical reports. The party elite has therefore devised a way to obtain the necessary empirical work while keeping the result within the party leadership so that it does not become public knowledge. The importance of this for the social sciences in the Soviet Union may be great in the long run, for having once recognized the need for empirical research and accurate measurements of social phenomena, the party is unlikely to be able to confine future research to such a narrow range and to non-empirical approaches.

Information obtained from cadres' experiences in political education and from investigations of the effectiveness of party work helps the leaders of the obkom, republic, and central party organs to determine the most useful methods and areas of emphasis in attempting to influence a particular group. A rather simple didactic approach, stressing current party policies and productive achievements, may be taken toward workers and peasants. The central problem of political education, however, seems to be presented by the intelligentsia. Towards them the approach may have to be more sophisticated and addressed to particular well-defined segments of the group. *Voprosy partii-*

nogo stroitel'stva records the wide use of seminars, "especially among scientific workers, school teachers, and engineers-technicians."[25] These seminars deal with philosophical problems and specific questions raised by science. The joint consideration of utilitarian and theoretical questions is evinced by the journal when it notes that "participants in the seminars not only master the current view on material of their science but are trained in the practical application of the principles and laws of dialectical materialism." Thus, a constant effort is made to synthesize the "practical" and the "philosophical." By linking the two, it is evidently hoped to win over members of the intelligentsia who may not spontaneously agree with some of the party's philosophical tenets. (Some lack of confidence in the attractiveness of its tenets is revealed by the heavily repetitious character of its efforts to persuade.) The combination also gives the party cadres grounds for asserting that the party has not only the wisdom but the right to take the lead in interpreting virtually all developments in all fields.

In Leningrad, the party organizes philosophical seminars for the intelligentsia in institutes of scientific research, secondary schools, and other educational establishments. The seminars are run collectively by bureaus of three to five cadres trained in advanced methods of political education.[26] The study of philosophic disciplines presents "dialectical and historical materialism, the science of Communism," as the most important foundation in forming the world view of the Soviet people. However, over half of those attending the seminars in Leningrad study economic questions. "The problem of equipping the masses, and especially the leading cadres, with deep economic knowledge is not temporary but continuing," according to official interpretation.[27] In short, the concern with productivity and technological advancement overlaps philosophic indoctrination and in some respects supersedes it in emphasis and importance.

Despite the apparently increasing emphasis on the practical

economic aspect of education, the Leningrad party organs still gave great attention to more traditional political instruction. In 1964, for example, 397,000 lectures were given by party cadres, of which 206,000 were on Marxist-Leninist theory. Innovation, science and technological subjects, and agriculture were the themes for over 48,000 of these lectures.[28] In addition, there were seminars and short courses on the history of the C.P.S.U. in which nearly 23,000 people participated in 1,344 courses; 16,674 participated in 923 seminars; and 9,732 attended 455 other seminars.[29] The source for these figures does not explain the differences between the seminars noted, but it can be assumed that they differed in the sophistication of their content. In 1964–1965 the total number of participants in political education in Leningrad purportedly passed one million.[30] Although far more lectures and seminars were given on party history and Marxist-Leninist thought, it should be noted that the economic education programs apparently had much larger attendance, for the claim is made that over half those who attended seminars studied economic questions.[31]

Starting from the revitalization program begun by the party leadership in the mid-1950's, the political education program spread nationally until by the mid-1960's it was directly reaching from 10 to 12 per cent of the total population of the U.S.S.R. In cities such as Leningrad and Moscow the percentage was two to three times higher. *Kommunist* reported that in 1960–1961 over 19 million, of whom 12.7 million were non-party, participated in the system of party education through lectures and seminars, and that in 1961–1962 over 22.5 million, of whom about 15.8 million were non-party, did so.[32] By 1964–1965, this figure had exceeded 26 million with an estimated 70 per cent of these non-party participants.[33] Assuming that these figures refer to different individuals, the data suggest that the party's direct (personal) political education program reaches 25 to 30 per cent of the total population of major urban areas but less than half that percentage in the country as a whole. This means that party seminars and lectures are either poorly attended in many of the towns, or that they are little used as means of reaching the non-urban population. The political education program thus seems to be in effect and perhaps in design as well to be focused largely on the city where the party already has its greatest numerical strength and organizational effectiveness.

INDUSTRIAL PROPAGANDA

The party's political education personnel and machinery were increasingly brought to bear on economic education during the 1955–1956 period, clearly with the functional aim of raising production and improving the quality of goods and services. The use of the party's propaganda and agitation cadres for this purpose required a retraining of many older cadres and the training of various types of production specialists in agit-prop techniques. These developments sparked in the party new controversy over the proper character of political education, the more orthodox arguing for heavy emphasis on history of the C.P.S.U. and Marxist-Leninist theory and the more pragmatic contending that "practical" economic education would yield more tangible and meaningful results. The pragmatically oriented therefore sought to use the instruments of political education as a means of promoting efficiency among the productive forces and enlarging the output of the economy. The fact that efficiency and output were largely within the purview of the state bureaucracy and industrial management created another area of conflict and further blurred the lines of responsibility between the various participants. Although the economic bureaucrats may generally agree with the more conservative apparatchiki who opposed the party's shift of interest from theory to production, the two groups differed significantly over the question of economic and technological specialization and the role of the specialist in the decision-making process. The more pragmatically minded apparatchiki were in general agreement with the economic bureaucrats on the role of specialists, but they disagreed on the role that the party should play in administration and management. It is probable that there are differences within each general group as well as between them, so that alignments shift periodically and new coalitions predominate until another dispute or combination of disputes leads to another realignment and policy adjustment.

One spur to the redevelopment of the party's political education program was the desire for specific results that could not be adequately promoted through the philosophical abstractions of Marxism-Leninism. *Partiinaia zhizn'* noted shortly after the 20th Party Congress that "party work is work with people, the organization and education of them, not aimless, abstract education. . . ."[34] The pejorative tone of the phrase "aimless, abstract education" suggests that the writer had found an excessive reliance on such forms of political training. In his estimation, the stress rather should be specific and should lead to tangible results. It was quickly seen by some party leaders that the development of this more practical form of political education could go hand in hand with the effort to revitalize the party after its years of disuse under Stalin and indeed could strengthen the party's position by making it a more efficient instrument of control and leadership. This view was suggested early in the revitalization program, for the article just cited in *Partiinaia zhizn'* went on to declare: "The more concretely and thoroughly party organizations occupy themselves with problems of economy, the quicker will they rid themselves of elements of rule by administrative fiat. . . ." While this statement can be interpreted in more than one way, the context indicates that economic and administrative efficiency should have priority and that the party, like the state, should rid itself of heavy-handed bureaucratic practices and measure results by efficiency and productivity.

That the growth of emphasis on practical economics evoked considerable controversy is revealed by a recent party-sponsored monograph in its effort to explain away the disagreement. *Voprosy ideologicheskoi raboty partii,* published for the Central Committee in 1966 by the Academy of Social Science, proclaims that "industrial propaganda has nothing in common either with abstract enlightenment or with narrow practicism and utilitarianism."[35] After thus declaring that both sides are wrong, the authors take the middle-of-the-road position that industrial propaganda "above all consists of that component of ideological work closely connected with production and having great educational significance," thereby allowing the importance of ideology but making clear that it is only one area of political education. The publication contends that, in addition to increasing knowledge in the areas of technical, economic, and organizational work, industrial propaganda "fosters conscious relations toward labor and explains its role in material production." This is considered especially significant because such education "trains workers to understand the relations of their work to the economics of the system and individual propaganda especially is directed to skilled workers and the activists among them as a means to strengthen labor discipline." One product of this approach has been schools of Communist labor that have been created as a form of mass "production education." Such schools are established in individual enterprises, scientific-research establishments, and project organizations, and on collective and state farms. Concentrated effort resulted in swelling the enrollment of these schools from 33,000 to 160,000 in the Leningrad oblast and from 10,800 to 115,200 in the Moscow city party organization during 1962–1964.[36] The use of such schools has purportedly increased since 1964. Although the Brezhnev-Kosygin regime rejected the "practicist-utilitarian" label, the continued development of schools of Communist labor and the general focus of industrial propaganda indicates that the name more than the aim has been repudiated. The party instruments of political education continue to emphasize production even though the style of the propaganda may be less flamboyant and overly optimistic than that of the Khrushchev period.

The Brezhnev leadership of the party apparatus has, however, criticized the conduct of industrial propaganda in an attempt to improve the party's efforts toward the economic education of the masses. The substance of this criticism is presented in *Voprosy ideologicheskoi raboty partii.* There were four charges. First, "several party organizations manifest excessive zeal" by presenting the people with too broad a program of economic education, not properly focusing it on their needs, and damaging the ideological content of the program by blurring the relationship of their particular work to the progress of the whole system.[37] Second, there is no system of transition from lower, beginning forms of instruction to higher, more advanced forms. Third, the beginning economic schools, circles, and seminars often differ from each other only in name and not in what is taught or what approach is used. And fourth, although many participants point out shortcomings in the way that economic circles and seminars relate concrete economics to production, few measures have been taken to remedy such weaknesses. This critical evaluation of industrial propaganda indicates rather clearly that the post-Khrushchev leadership intends to improve the system of economic education through political means rather than to abandon it. The desire reflected by all four observations appears to be almost entirely to improve the efficiency and effectiveness of party education.

MASS COMMUNICATIONS AND POLITICAL EDUCATION

The Soviet publicist is "above all a propagandist of ideas and of the practical problems of building Communism."[38] The candor of such statements often surprises the Western observer of the

Soviet system, but the Soviet mass communications media are quite openly designed to perform a propaganda function and the party leaders do not consider the word *propaganda* a term of oprobrium. The party itself, of course, plays a major role in determining the pattern and content of the written, spoken, and visual materials employed by mass communications media.

The solid work done on the Soviet system by such scholars as Frederick Barghoorn renders unnecessary any detailed description of the use of mass communication and the educational system as instruments of political socialization.[39] Rather than duplicate the work of others, the present writer here offers a few general observations.

While the party maintains its own press, the party schools also train editors for the general press, radio, and television. The Higher Party School, for example, has developed special programs to train such editors. In 1962, the Central Committee instructed the State Committee on Radio and Television to work with republic central committees and councils of ministers in improving programming and in developing new "skilled cadres with good understanding of radio and television."[40] They were to train thirty to thirty-five propagandists annually in the Higher Party School and up to a hundred editors in the republic and oblast party schools. This method provides the party with generally reliable personnel to direct the Soviet communications media and enables it to coordinate their professional training and enculcate common professional values and expectations.

It is easier for the party to give close supervision to large mass communications media than to small ones. *Pravda* and its republic and urban counterparts, *Trud*, and central broadcasting and telecasting stations are relatively easy to control. Uniform standards are more difficult to impose upon local and professional publications. Consequently, there is some diversity in the local press and some independence in professional publications such as *Novy mir* and in small and middle-sized general ones such as *Yunost*. The genuinely mass press, however, is rigorously controlled. The differences that occasionally appear, especially in editorials of *Pravda, Izvestiia, Krasnaia zvezda,* and *Sovetskaia rossia* are probably too subtle for the average Soviet citizen to detect.

Over the mass media, the party unquestionably exercises effective negative control—what is not to be published or broadcast—as well as a positive control that promotes desired patterns of behavior and thought. However, the key question of how effective are these mass political socialization programs cannot be adequately answered at the present time. C.P.S.U. officials are also interested and have instigated some surveys, but the results have been made public in only a few instances.

In the Leningrad oblast, for example, some fragmentary evidence has been published. Assuming the accuracy of the data released, there were in 1965 thirty publishers and a department of central publishers in the oblast. The Radio and Television Committee had about 200 editors. There were reportedly 700,000 television sets and 1,250,000 radio receiver sets available to the people in the oblast.[41] There were 135 newspapers with a total circulation of 1.2 million copies; the largest was *Leningradskaia Pravda* with a circulation of 350,000, followed by *Vecherny Leningrad* with 135,000.[42] Among young attendants at a chemical plant, the survey found that 22.4 per cent in 1962–1963 studied questions of current politics; in 1963–1964 the figure was 24.5 per cent; and under a propaganda campaign to increase the number it was hoped that 56 per cent would study such questions in 1967. Of those who fell in the 24.5 per cent in 1963–1964, 85.9 per cent professed to read political journals and 95.7 per cent said they read newspapers.[43] Neither the number of workers participating nor the questions used to determine awareness of current politics were reported. The means of influencing the populace are clearly present but the character and depth of the influence have not been adequately studied and reported.

Another interesting and important question concerns the motivation of individuals who attend the seminars and lectures and read party journals and newspapers. Many of them, of course, may do so with no ulterior motives whatsoever. It is also possible, and in the opinion of this author quite likely, that attendance at party programs and study of party literature are used by some as means of personal advancement. When political education is as important to the leadership as it is in the Soviet Union, it is only to be expected that some individuals will exploit that importance to their own advantage.

EDUCATION AND ELECTIONS

One of the striking differences between the Soviet system and most Western systems is that electoral processes in the U.S.S.R. are more appropriately considered as part of political socialization than as an aspect of political recruitment. In addition to the lack of choice among candidates, a reason for considering the electoral process and the activities of Soviets as part of the political socialization process is the concerted effort made by the party officials and members to use the occasions to influence non-party persons.

"The non-party are especially cultivated at election time," one Soviet work declares.[44] It goes on to note that in 1963 about 6 million of 8,588,150 workers in the electoral process were non-party. The elections therefore serve a multiple purpose. They draw a large number of people directly into the process through the election commissions. They also create an opportunity for an official campaign, in which leaders and local candidates may personally address large numbers of citizens with speeches attuned to current political education motifs. And, last, elections may provide a sense of participation in the country's political processes even though formal choices are negligible and the actual power of deputies is virtually non-existent.

Over 2 million deputies are elected to the various levels of soviets. Of these about 45 per cent are party members.[45] The percentage of party members is much higher for the republic and all-union soviets and often lower for the local and provincial soviets. For the non-party deputies, membership in the soviets is regarded as a learning experience. It is the responsibility of the party group in each soviet to help non-party deputies "improve their political knowledge and learn Marxist theory in order to co-ordinate their activities with those of the party. . . . Deputy Communists, guides of the political party in the soviets, [also] encourage union with electors, respond sensitively to their daily needs."[46] The responsibility of the party groups is frankly stated to be the attainment of "even broader and fuller use of all forms of mass social control through the work of the soviets."[47] The integration into the political processes of the non-party deputy, who is usually a person in a position of some importance, is aided by appointing such deputies to standing commissions. The integrative process itself is then broadened when the support of activist citizens who are not deputies is enlisted by giving them assignments, however small, with the standing commissions.[48] The whole process may consequently be described as another effort to achieve integration through a participatory form of political socialization.

THE C.P.S.U. AND THE TRAINING OF YOUTH

Nowhere is the regime's lack of confidence in its ability to win spontaneous and genuine support more clearly revealed than in its official youth organizations and institutions of public education. From the Little Octobrists to the Young Pioneers to the Komsomols to the public schools, party activists constantly seek to form and to reinforce the official pattern of attitudes and values. The scope of the party's efforts and the didacticism of its approach is illustrated by the following quotation from *Kom-*

somolskaia Pravda, which is taken from a directive to the editors of 164 Young Communist League (Y.C.L.) publications with a reported circulation in 1957 of over 13 million.

> Our task is to instill in young people a deep ideological spirit, selfless love for the socialist homeland, proletarian internationalism, a love of work, collectivism and comradeship; to inculcate in them a modern scientific outlook, atheism and a spirit of struggle against religious prejudices; in every way to support and propagandize the beginnings of everything new and Communist. Y.C.L. organizations must bring up the younger generation to be cheerful, buoyant, healthy and industrious, with a high sense of responsibility for the fate of their fatherland and prepared at the first call of the Party to defend their homeland. All ideological work in Y.C.L. organizations must be closely linked with the practical work of building Communism and subordinated to the tasks of successfully carrying out the historic decisions of the 20th Party Congress.[49]

This approach indicates the party's concern both with values and with behavior patterns. In the area of attitudes and values Communist youth must be taught Marxist-Leninist theory and "all forms and methods of party propaganda."[50] In the area of behavior patterns young Communists must learn and pursue the goals of the party with unrelenting enthusiasm. The party proclaims its reliance on youth "for the introduction of new techniques and progressive technology, the study and dissemination of advanced experiments, the promotion of productive work, struggle against waste, aid to young workers, the control of economic activities, and many other things."[51] This promotion of production-oriented goals is designed to advance the integration of the populace in the effort to attain national aspirations.

The inculcation of achievement values begins in earnest in the training of Young Pioneers. *Pravda* noted that among the chief problems in political education confronted by troop leaders of the Young Pioneers is the one of inspiring "publicly useful labor and labor education."[52] The same article reported that trade unions were beginning to help organize Young Pioneer activities as a means of meeting the challenge. However, despite their conscious effort to promote achievement values, the ability of youth leaders to focus solely on such problems should not be over-estimated. Allen Kassof, in his work *The Soviet Youth Program*, observes, "if one examines the actual behavior of the Pioneers and the Komsomol, then it is soon evident that the activities making up the youth program are, with few exceptions, quite ordinary. . . ." He goes on to say that the activities "would be familiar to any American who has attended a public school or belonged to a Boy Scout troop."[53]

Of the youth organizations, the Komsomol is the most immediately useful to the C.P.S.U. Recognizing this, the party maintains a close association with the Y.C.L. through an extensive network of Komsomol officials who are simultaneously active party members. Party control stems from the C.P.S.U. Central Committee, extends through the Y.C.L. apparatus and Central Committee, and goes on to include the staffs of local Y.C.L. organizations.

The total membership of the Komsomol reached 23 million in 1965.[54] Brief examination of the Leningrad Komsomol organization illustrates the backgrounds of the members and their relationship with the C.P.S.U. In 1965, the Leningrad Y.C.L. had 513,000 members. Of these, 168,000 were workers, 100,000 were employees, 242,000 were students, and 1,750 were kolkhozniki.[55] Although the percentage that were already members or candidate members of the party is not available, it was reported that 4,000 C.P.S.U. members and candidates worked in the Leningrad Komsomol apparatus and that over 600 of these were secretaries of various Y.C.L. organs.[56] This figure probably includes a large percentage, perhaps nearly all, of those who worked in the apparatus of the Y.C.L. in Leningrad.

According to Kassof, the activities of the Komsomols fall into five chief categories: "education, socialist competition, surveillance, checking on management, and labor recruitment."[57] All of these have instrumental objectives in that they are designed to secure the maintenance of the system and to stimulate efficiency and productivity. Whether or not they accomplish these objectives, the point here is that this is their aim. Also, in all five areas, the Y.C.L. is an agency complementary to the party, rather than an independent support for the C.P.S.U.

In the field of political and economic education, Komsomol activities parallel those of the party except that they cater more to a young audience. The activities of the Moscow gorkom of the Komsomol illustrate this point. Three faculties of the gorkom prepare future propagandists, lecturers, and debate leaders who specialize in mass work with youth in political and cultural areas. In addition, the yearly program of the Moscow Komsomol includes frequent debates, theoretical conferences, discussion sessions, and similar open meetings in an attempt to reinforce certain values and to stimulate interest in party programs.[58]

Despite the constant effort to socialize young people into accepting certain normative patterns of behavior, there are frequent references in the Soviet press to failures and problems. Most of these references fall into one of two categories: (1) complaints about the behavior of young people and their failure to live up to the normative and moral ideals formulated by the party and (2) complaints about the difficulties encountered by the C.P.S.U. and the Y.C.L. in exercising effective leadership in the education system, particularly in institutions of higher learning. *Partiinaia zhizn'* commented that "in some higher educational institutions things have reached the point where not only Communists but even secretaries of party committees have ceased to attend Y.C.L. meetings and have basically lost contact with the youth."[59]

Almost invariably signs of apathy or hostility to official guidelines are explained as the result of poor ideological-educational work and the failure of party guidance in some Y.C.L. organizations and institutions of higher learning. Rarely are specific sociological or economic problems blamed for "unorthodox" behavior, although failure to gain admission to a particular institution of higher learning or to obtain a particular kind of job has been advanced as a cause for some of this behavior.[60] More often it is simply reported that "individual students have been exposed to unhealthy sentiments and from time to time yield to the influences of an alien ideology," without explanation of where these influences originate and how they happen to have found adherents in the Soviet Union.[61] On September 9, 1966, a *Pravda* editorial on the situation included the criticism that "the party bodies of some republics and provinces have slackened their attention to ideological-upbringing work among students and have lowered their demands on the agencies that guide educational institutions and on party and Y.C.L. organizations of higher and specialized secondary educational institutions." The proposed solution was for the party and the Y.C.L. to "intensify their control" over secondary and higher educational institutions and to raise the level of social science instruction. Such steps are the antidote commonly advocated when the problem is mentioned.

The party's concern and control over the processes of overt political socialization have probably increased rather than diminished in the post-Stalin period for two major reasons. First, emphasis on political socialization was commonly (and probably quite correctly) viewed as a necessary compensation for the diminution in terror: the process is seen as a means of control over the masses. Second, technological improvements in mass communications made a centrally directed program of continuous and massive political education both possible and potentially very effective. A third possible factor was the practical benefit that might have been expected to accrue from the use of socialization to raise the morale and technical proficiency of economically productive sectors of the population.

Despite the emphasis given political socialization, major problems continue to undermine its effectiveness. The didactic method, for example, may become tedious, boring, or meaningless to those who must hear the same expressions and pleas repeated day after day. In time, didacticism may degenerate into contradictory oversimplifications and encourage at least the intellectually astute to question the whole process. Such an approach probably wears thin quickly on university campuses and in other circles of learning. Indications are that something of the sort has come about in the Soviet Union and that didactic repetition may ultimately weaken the effectiveness of overt indoctrination rather than to build loyalty and active support. Another principal problem arises from the almost complete lack of confidence in spontaneous socialization of a sort acceptable to the party, which leads to over-organization of the means of socialization. This weakness is most manifest in the complex arrangement of lectures, seminars, circles, conferences, and so forth, that Soviet citizens are expected to attend. Not only does this result in duplication of effort and wasted man-hours, but it can lead to the frustration of individuals who enter such programs sincerely wishing to improve their knowledge and skills. The inclination to over-do rather than the inability to communicate and persuade is what may jeopardize the effectiveness of the party's direction of the overt processes of political socialization.

The C.P.S.U. and Goal Specification

All political parties have certain goals that their leaders must articulate and help to attain. The processes for specifying these goals, however, vary drastically among individual parties and party systems. Probably the organization and functions of the C.P.S.U. and Communist parties in power differ most radically from other parties in the means by which goals are determined and in the authority that the goals carry.

From the outset of the Bolshevik regime the party elite took precedence over the formal government in making major policy decisions for the country. The members of the Politburo, the Central Committee, and, to a lesser extent, the party congresses dealt with the principal policy problems. Although some members of the Politburo also held government posts, their positions were primarily organizational and administrative. The possibility that a government ministry might develop interests of its own and become a base of independent political power for its incumbents was not officially recognized early in the Soviet period, except perhaps by such bureaucratic strategists as Stalin himself. During the Stalin period, the party organs declined as effective agents of policy. Especially during World War II, a small cabinet of Stalin's most trusted and effective lieutenants superseded the party organs in initiating and executing policy. The ability of the dictator to impose his own personal policies and to select his own advisers and lieutenants enabled him to disregard the "party legality" of the early 1920's. Even then, however, clusters of economic, administrative, and ideological interests maintained pockets of political strength. Stalin sometimes accepted the demands of such groups but he also often played one against the other in order to neutralize them. Perhaps his most effective strategy for dealing with such interest aggregations was to deny them any regular procedure for bringing their petitions to the top leadership. There simply was no ready access to Stalin and his confidants through personal or organizational channels.

The Second World War necessitated more constant communications and a dependable inflow of information. Although the previous rapid industrialization had seen the beginning of regular lines of communication between important economic and administrative units and the nation's policy-makers, the war made their complete development mandatory if the regime was to survive. An important political result of this was to elevate a small coterie of the Council of Ministers to preeminence among the party's decision-makers, including the Politburo. It was hardly surprising then that for nearly two years Malenkov was able to lead the regime from the Premiership without having any formal authority over the party apparatus.

The Khrushchev years saw the party revived and efforts made to establish its supremacy in policy-making and administrative leadership. This development naturally sparked conflict between the party and elements of the state bureaucracy that had attained political power and some independence under Stalin and Malenkov. Khrushchev's attempts to shift the focus of the party from ideology to economic leadership not only sharpened conflict over policy among the ruling elite and heightened tension between party and state (especially in the field of agriculture), but also exacerbated the problem of determining which organ took precedence in resolving disputes. At various times the Politburo, the Central Committee, the First Secretary himself, the Council of Ministers, the Presidium of the Council of Ministers, and combinations of these appeared responsible for approving policy. Yet no precise jurisdiction was ever marked, although the Politburo in most instances seemed to prevail. As long as the higher party organs confined themselves largely to general policy-making, this arrangement may have worked adequately if not very efficiently; but once the party elite began to intervene on a large scale in economic management and middle- and low-range economic decisions, the procedural question of who had the right to make policy and who had the responsibility for implementing it assumed growing importance. This became one of the major conflicts of the Khrushchev period and weighed heavily in his removal from power.

Such procedural turmoil contributes largely to two of the most serious political difficulties faced by the C.P.S.U. and the Soviet government: the problems of succession and leadership and of resolving policy conflict through well-defined processes. Soviet-ologists have written much on the succession and leadership problem but only recently has the post-Stalin policy conflict been given serious study.[1] It should be remarked that the two problems are inextricably linked and both demand a procedural solution. Indeed, conflict over succession and leadership may be held to be irreconcilable without an institutionalzed procedure for reaching decisions. A legitimate way to resolve policy conflicts must precede the legitimation of leadership or at least be part of the same or a similar process, so closely related are the question of power and the problem of defining issues.

Policy conflicts between left-right, dogmatist-revisionist cleavages in the party have been historically accompanied by division and personnel changes among the members of the Politburo and the Central Committee. Membership changes, expecially during the Stalin period, were often attended by purges and extreme punishment of the losers. The post-Stalin period has been notably marked by the restraint of the victors in dealing with their opponents. Demotions, appointments to other and often distant positions, and retirements have been the penalties for siding with a losing faction, but even more importantly the losing group has never entirely lost its representation in the Politburo since Stalin's death, with the single exception of the so-called anti-party group of 1957—and even that required four years to effect. In that case, furthermore, the conflict concerned the party leadership and was not confined to disagreement over policy. In part, the absence of broad scale purges has been due, as Carl Linden suggests, to agreement among Stalin's successors to abandon the practice, but it has also resulted from the failure of a single leader or even a single coalition to muster the power to dispose of opposition.[2] In short, since 1953 majority coalitions have been tenuous and have fluctuated in composition according to the political exigencies of the moment.

Reflecting the struggle over both leadership and policy, the membership of the Politburo has changed often since the 19th Party Congress in 1952. There were periods of relative stability between 1953 and mid-1957 when officials from the government bureaucracy predominated in the Politburo, and between mid-1957 and May 1960 when party apparatchiki were predominant. Since 1960, there has been a tenuous balance between state and party officials, with the apparatchiki usually holding a slight numerical advantage. Such categorizing only partially indicates the relative standing of the groups, of course, for some bureaucrats have had considerable experience in the party apparatus and some apparatchiki are specialists in various technical aspects of production. The bureaucrat-apparatchiki division is useful primarily for identifying the base of power and the current professional associations of members of the Politburo.

The composition of the Politburo is known, but the internal operations of that policy-making organ remain a mystery. Khrushchev referred briefly to the conduct of meetings, noting that issues were discussed, an attempt was made to reach a consensus, and a majority vote prevailed if no consensus could be reached. A report of the U.S. Senate entitled *Staffing Procedures and Problems in the Soviet Union* asserts that the Politburo is divided into "teams" that "are probably the primary policy formulators in various spheres."[3] These teams reportedly include specialists in key policy areas. The study claims that not only do members and candidate members of the Politburo serve on the teams but that "outside" key specialists, such as the Minister of Foreign Affairs and the Minister of Defense, often attend the committee sessions. All of the non-members of the Politburo listed as participating in team operations were members of the Central Committee.

Global Policy Issues		*Party Issues*	
Military & Intelligence	Diplomacy & Trade	International Communism	Domestic Party Affairs

Domestic Economic Issues	
Industry	Agriculture

The Central Committee, as discussed in Chapter II, has a less active but still important role to play. The members serve as major communications channels both to and from the Politburo. The Politburo alone normally makes policy, but when its members are undecided or evenly divided, the Central Committee may have considerable influence on the final decision. Even when the Committee is not in session, certain of its members are probably in communication with one of the working committees of the Politburo.

The information needed to make effective operational decisions comes from a network of sources. The composition of this network is party a reflection of the Central Committee, but it is not confined to that body. Party members in government ministries, planning organs, the military officer corps, the scientific community, and other specialized agencies of the system often are in touch with the party elite. Provincial secretaries of the party are major sources of information, for they administer the party's control over culture and economy and often are involved in the administration of agricultural policy. Through its own structure and through its members who hold key non-party positions, the party policy-makers gather information about problem areas in order to make better-informed decisions. However, the same access to persons holding specialized positions and representing specialized groups also opens the policy process somewhat to the influence of the information sources. That gradually took place during the post-Stalin period. This development has meant that group interests and their advancement have become a part of the political system. In turn, policy conflict has been sharpened to some extent among the members of the higher party organs as they have been constantly exposed to different points of view and have had to reconcile different orders of priorities.

GOALS AND PRIORITIES, 1956–1966

In order to identify and evaluate the goals and pattern of priorities established by the party elite between 1956 and 1966, the speeches delivered at party congresses by leading party officials and the editorials of *Pravda* were subjected to content analysis. The speeches examined were those given by members of the Politburo and Secretariat before the 20th, 21st, 22nd, and 23rd Congresses of the C.P.S.U. The editorials selected for examination were those published every other Monday and Thursday during even-numbered years. Both quantitative and qualitative methods were employed in the following presentation and analysis of our findings.

Table I presents a quantitative assessment of selected goals taken from those advanced in the speeches of party leaders at the four party Congresses. The figures were obtained by a count of key phrases, adjusted to reflect the number of speeches studied. Khrushchev's secret speech is not included since it dealt largely with historical matters. Part A of Table I records the key party problems that were emphasized. Part B lists the frequency with which economic and cultural problems were treated.

TABLE I
Goals Specified at Party Congresses

Part A

	20th Cong.	21st Cong.	22nd Cong.	23rd Cong.
Party leadership of society	11	11	29	10
Party ideological work	13	15	13	12
Collective leadership	9	2	11	2
Abolition of cult of personality	9	3	42	0
Growth in party membership	1	2	4	6
Recruitment of specialists	6	8	1	6

Part B

	20th Cong.	21st Cong.	22nd Cong.	23rd Cong.
Agricultural management	9	17	21	18
Light industry management	9	10	19	22
Heavy industry management	18	15	20	26
Priority of heavy industry	17	12	3	2
Role of & need for specialists	28	15	7	8
Cultural problems & goals (especially education)	5	9	8	14

Part of the evidence of goal priorities which emerged from content analysis of *Pravda* editorials is given in Table II. The figures are presented without adjustment. Tables I and II together with some additional evidence are analyzed topically in the following section.

TABLE II

Goals Specified in PRAVDA *Editorials*

	1956	1958	1960	1962	1964	1966
Party leadership of society	24	13	4	14	14	10
Party ideological work	3	4	2	10	1	9
Party as leader of production	8	6	2	4	2	6
Recruitment of specialists	1	6	2	2	1	1
Management of economy	22	27	28	10	17	28
Priority of heavy industry	12	6	7	2	0	0
Role of & need for specialists	7	12	6	7	20	13
Cultural problems & goals	8	9	6	7	3	13

PARTY LEADERSHIP

Organizational and methodological goals of the party received considerable attention during the decade following 1956, remaining relatively constant for the lower levels of the party but varying significantly for the higher levels. The lower levels focused on both organization and methods, but the concern at higher levels was largely for methods or procedures, aside from the controversy that followed Khrushchev's effort to reorganize sections of the party in 1962.

The addresses of party leaders before the congresses of the C.P.S.U. differed markedly from the editorials of *Pravda* during the Khrushchev period. The party congress speeches tried to establish basic principles of leadership at the higher levels of the party. The principle of collective leadership and the call for "abolition of the cult of personality," were frequent themes in the speeches, but such matters were mentioned only incidentally in *Pravda*. Two explanations for this discrepancy may be hazarded: (1) factions in the Politburo, Secretariat, and Central Committee exploited both issues, collective leadership and the cult of personality, in the struggle for power, and (2) the leadership feared that both issues could be exploited by lesser elites if given too much publicity.

References to collective leadership were more frequent during the 20th Congress, when Khrushchev was moving to consolidate his position and to weaken his opponents, and during the 22nd Congress, when Khrushchev appeared to have reached a workable dual power arrangement. The 22nd Congress was exceptional for its numerous references to collective leadership, abolition of the cult of personality, and enhancement of the party's position of leadership in Soviet society—such references were sharply higher than in either the preceding or the succeeding congresses. The resurrection of the 1957 anti-party group as an issue is part of the explanation, but the resurgence of the conservative faction under Frol Kozlov was also a factor. Toward the end of the Congress Khrushchev himself delivered a most interesting colloquy on party leadership, apparently intended both as a defense of his own leadership and a condemnation of his critics. He declared that the anti-party group had sought to reinstitute outmoded methods of administration developed under the cult of the individual. Roundly condemning the cult of personality, he cited numerous cases of injustice during the great purges and called for every leader to be strictly accountable to party control, a principle he asserted to be perverted by the cult of the individual. Then, in a very unusual comment, Khrushchev deprecated his own role and claimed that governmental and party policy decisions were made collectively. He tried to strike a balance in his argument between the principle of a leader's authority and his responsibility to the collective body of leadership. In contrast, deliberations at the 23rd Congress did not refer to the cult of personality and the few incidental mentions of collective leadership took the principle for granted, as requiring neither defense nor definition.

The goal of party leadership in Soviet society is one for which the party leaders have assumed general acceptance among the people, but they have differed among themselves as to the specific form that leadership should take. For example, during the Khrushchev period, old-line government bureaucrats and the new breed of specialists in the party apparatus diverged sharply in their views of how the party should exercise its leadership of the economy. The more positive and complete the economic role advocated for the party apparatchiki, the less secure and more antagonistic became leaders of the economic bureaucracy. The controversy on the role of the party leadership in production as well as in other fields is revealed by the rise and fall of references in *Pravda:* they were frequent in 1956 as Khrushchev was preparing his assault on the bureaucracy, declined after his victory over the anti-party group, and bounced back in 1962 and 1964 when he again was attacked by the more conservative, neo-Stalinist forces of the party. This increase is paralleled by the sharply increased attention given the issue in the 22nd Party Congress.

The slant of *Pravda* editorials greatly illuminates the development of the party leadership issue. On February 20, 1956, the *growing* leadership of the party in all facets of economic development was cited. On March 5, great importance was attached to the party's setting up of structures to guide the development of the national economy, and the need for structural adaptations and training of qualified party personnel was stressed. During both the Khrushchev and Brezhnev periods, the editorials focused their attention on activating the local party organizations and elevating their roles, especially their economic responsibilities. The editorial of July 26, 1962, is typical. It speaks of the smallest party groups as important leaders and educators of the masses in the struggle to build the material-technical basis for Communism; and it praises their intimate involvement with the immediate details of production. Carrying this theme further, the editorial of February 7, 1966, declared that the main tasks of party organs are the organization and supervision of economic life and the education of the public in Communist ideology.

Despite differences over managerial questions, the C.P.S.U. elite consistently assumed a major share of the economic leadership. Indeed, their responsibility in that sector seems to have increased rather than decreased during the decade under consideration. It may be contended, then, that the party sought to maintain its effective leadership in Soviet society primarily by expanding its role in the crucial economic sphere. Whatever erosion or reduction of leadership the party might suffer in various subsystems, such as the military or the literary, it would more than compensate by extending its control over the economy on which all subdivisions of the system were in some way dependent.

GOALS CONCERNING SPECIALIZATION AND IDEOLOGY

The training and recruitment of specialists and the role of ideology will be examined together here primarily because the party in recent years has tended to emphasize "practical ideological work" and the close relation of such work to the problem of recruiting specialists. The absence of any significant variation on either issue between the Khrushchev and Brezhnev periods of party leadership also enables us to consider both goals simultaneously.

In discussing the need for specialization in his address to the 20th Party Congress, Khrushchev underscored three problems that have had the continued attention of his successors. First, he called for more careful planning for the training of specialists in specific managerial duties. By this he implied that technical specialists should be groomed for managerial responsibilities over that aspect of production in which they are expert. Second, he stressed the need for increased communication between the scientific community and producers in order to bring science to bear on practical production problems. Third, he criticized the party's ideological work for being too divorced from "the practical realities of production" and called for the ideological training of the young to put greater stress on practical applications. Suslov echoed this last point by declaring, "It is the duty of all party organizations . . . to ensure a sharp turn in our ideological work toward life, toward practice. . . ."

The year 1958 was marked by a stepped-up campaign to improve the quality of specialists' training in line with Khrushchev's recommendations at the 20th Party Congress. *Pravda* gave the question considerable space. Noting that increased mechanization and efficiency of production required more specialists, its editorials called for more technical and practical education in all Soviet schools and for the training of increased numbers of specialists for all branches of the economy.[4] The "greatest attention," however, was given to quantity rather than quality, for enough specialists had to be educated to meet "the increasing needs of the economy."[5] *Pravda* for October 3, 1966, sounded a similar note. Concern for this matter continued into the 1960's as the party program called for increased numbers of both higher and middle educational institutions to prepare specialists.[6] This problem was linked closely with the recruitment of party apparatchiki in Nikolai Podgorny's speech to the 22nd Party Congress. He cited the success of trained specialists as party cadres and their importance in the implementation of economic goals. Brezhnev returned to the theme at the 23rd Congress, promising that the party would continue to press specialist training as a source of leaders and cadres in all phases of economic, state, and party work. - cont. here

Improved relations between scientists and production leaders also continued to be a party objective. The *Pravda* editorial of December 3, 1956, called for party members to take the initiative in coordinating science and industry and for specialists to undertake the introduction of scientific and technological advances into field work.[7] At the 23rd Congress, Brezhnev emphasized the importance of transforming science into a "direct productive force."

Attention given to ideological questions remained remarkably constant at all four congresses. In the editorials of *Pravda*, however, there was a marked increase of references to ideological issues in 1958 and 1964, as well as in the first quarter of 1968.

The principal ideological issue during 1956–1966 was that of relating ideology to the practical work of expanding Soviet production. Toward this end, ideological work was put to two general uses. In one, ideological training was used to improve technical knowledge and proficiency among Soviet workers and farmers. This required the training of large numbers of technical specialists who could then be recruited as party leaders and cadres. In the other, Marxist-Leninist ideology and the "new Soviet man" approach to it was used to inculcate strong spiritual commitment among Soviet citizens to fulfilling and exceeding specific productive goals. The two uses of ideology were combined, as usual, in the *Pravda* editorial on December 22, 1966. It declared that party ideological work chiefly should be to carry out the decision of the 23rd Congress: that is, to train workers so as to build in them a Communist consciousness and a sense of responsibility toward the practical objectives set by the party.

INDUSTRIAL PRIORITIES

One of the principal issues of the post-Stalin period was whether heavy industry should continue to receive the priority in industrial development and resource allocation signified by the catchword inherited from the Stalin era, "the preponderant growth of heavy industry." Malenkov, during his brief interregnum as Prime Minister, incurred the opposition of traditionalists by suggesting that, despite Leninist theory, the preponderance was no longer essential. He was compelled to yield on this issue, but the question had been raised and in modified form later found its way into Khrushchev's program.

At the time of the 20th Party Congress, heavy industry was still the predominant problem in resource allocations. Khrushchev, in using the issue to attack Malenkov, was led to defend the preponderant growth of heavy industry with a zeal that he must have later regretted. Even then, however, he entered a qualification: ". . . while continuing to maintain rapid development of heavy industry, we can and must at the same time expand the scope of development of consumer goods production." It was nonetheless clear from other references in Khrushchev's speech and from the editorials of *Pravda* that the policy of the party leadership was to give priority in allocations to heavy industry and that growth of the rest of the economy would be incidental. On July 16, 1956, *Pravda* declared that heavy industry was the present and future "basis of all increases in national wealth and popular welfare."

After the reorganization of the economic bureaucracy in 1957, there were increasing indications that the doctrine of the preponderant growth of heavy industry was becoming more selectively administered. Certain areas of heavy industry, especially machine tools and diversified forms of instrumentation, could make a larger, or at least a more immediate, contribution to production. This growing understanding of the advantages and limitations of various facets of industry gradually gave rise to discrimination in place of the former wholesale and indiscriminant endorsement of the preponderant growth of heavy industry. References to this traditional theme declined markedly in congresses after the 20th as well as in *Pravda*. After 1964, this once "basic tenet" of Soviet Marxism was mentioned only infrequently and incidentally.

Both the *Pravda* editorials and the speeches delivered at party congresses indicated that the leadership was seeking to expand agricultural and consumer-goods production in a way that would placate the champions of heavy industry—they stressed the prerequisite role of heavy industry in providing the machinery and machine tools required for mass production. Thus, heavy industry could legitimately be presented as the basis for economic growth, and conflicts between heavy and light industry could be considered irrelevant. The two types of industry were intertwined. Nevertheless, the party leaders appeared in fact to be shifting emphasis to a moderate but genuine consumer orientation with the expressed goal, "light industry production meets consumer demand."[8]

MANAGERIAL PROBLEMS AND GOALS

Management and industrial efficiency are persistent problems in the Soviet Union, and each new leadership has had to grapple with them soon after attaining power. Every major period of Soviet development has been marked by reorganization and experimentation, such as the shift from war Communism to the centralized command economy under Stalin. Khrushchev attempted to modify Stalin's rigid system with a partial decentralization, and his successors have tried to strike a balance between Stalin's policy and Khrushchev's experiments. References during the 1956–1966 decade to managerial problems and goals were most frequent during the 1956–1958 reforms and the 1964–1966 reorganization. The increase during the last two years of Khrushchev's leadership gives evidence that organizational and managerial issues provided opponents of the former First Secretary with some of their chief points of attack.

Khrushchev began his reorganization program with partial decentralization of the agricultural and industrial bureaucracies and the simultaneous enlargement of the party's role in economic management. Both aspects were politically loaded issues and aroused opposition from the beginning, for it was never clear whether Khrushchev's real aim was to place greater authority and initiative in the hands of regional managers under the tutelage of party cadres or to weaken the power base of those government ministers who opposed him. In any event, the replacement of numerous national ministries with new regional economic councils and the expanded use of trained specialists as party cadres with enlarged responsibilities for economic supervision were never fully accepted by all members of the party elite even at the height of Khrushchev's power.

The programs of Khrushchev's successors have differed more in style and general approach than in substance. The recent shift toward (not to) a market economy and the encouragement of limited initative on the part of local management had their antecedents in the Khrushchev regime. However, unlike Khrushchev's sometimes hastily conceived and implemented programs, the Brezhnev-Kosygin leadership has seemed more concerned with the rational development of long-term economic reforms. There has been a marked absence of bold promises to cure all ills immediately. Aside from approach, the greatest difference between the two leaderships has been the restoration of centralized management and planning. The Brezhnev-Kosygin government abolished the regional economic councils and reestablished central economic ministries. Their general efforts seem to have been toward balancing central control and planning on the one hand with an incentive system of competition and limited initiative by local management on the other. Whether such a balance is possible is not in our province here.

At the 23rd Party Congress, Brezhnev set forth the party's goals in economic management and the reasons for discontinuing some of Khrushchev's experiments. He claimed that economic growth had been hindered by poor administration and planning, lack of economic accountability, and the lack of material and moral incentives. The party's economic principles, he argues, called for ". . . strengthening the role of economic methods and incentives in the management of the national economy, in radically improving state planning, in broadening the independence and initiative of enterprises and collective and state farms, and in increasing the responsibility of production collectives and their material interest in the results of their activity." Brezhnev argues that centralized management of separate industries was preferable because Khrushchev's territorial method had resulted in violation of uniform technical standards. Such remarks at the 23rd Congress and commentaries on the preparation of the new economic plan in 1966 indicated the greater importance attached to industrial centralization. On February 24 and March 10, *Pravda* claimed that the reorganization of management in industry would facilitate better planning. On June 6, *Pravda* called on the party to exert stronger management and leadership of the economy. The premise seemed to be that intelligent centralization would result in more effective supervision by the elite and also in greater efficiency and productivity.

A principal question that remained unanswered by the Brezhnev-Kosygin leadership was how party leadership of the economy would be exerted. The reestablishment of central ministerial bureaucracies in the economic sector could cause disruptive conflict between career managers in the state bureaucracy and party cadres trained and experienced as economic overlords. It could also lead to eventual assimilation of the two groups of managerial technocrats, submerging formal institutional attachments in a sea of common practical interests. If that were to happen, how would the party justify its existence independent of the state? The goals of the bureaucrat and the apparatchiki would become indistinguishable.

GOALS OF PRODUCTIVITY

Of all the economic goals of the party, none has been more persistently emphasized from the beginning than that of a general and continuing increase in production. Indeed, this goal is undoubtedly shared by the dominant parties in all developing regimes. In the U.S.S.R., the cold war sharpened the urgency of the objective by holding up the productive capacity of the United States as the target that should be met and then surpassed. Also, the danger of thermonuclear war probably led Soviet leaders to emphasize economic competition as the most reasonable alternative to a revolutionary and high-risk foreign policy.

In his address to the 22nd Party Congress, Khrushchev developed a theme that had become his trademark in the field of economic growth. It was that improvement in the productivity of labor was the point on which to concentrate in economic development. He claimed that nine-tenths of the planned increase in industrial production could be achieved through increasing labor productivity. The pacesetters were to be the party members and party organizations: they "must be in the vanguard of development of all phases of production." At the same congress, Kosygin called for fuller use of available equipment and better organization of labor to increase productivity. He made similar demands at the 23rd Party Congress. The *Pravda* editorials pertaining to this subject repeatedly stressed the party leadership's desire to improve labor productivity through better organization and greater application of automation and other forms of technology. In 1964 and 1966, the editorials voiced a concern for quality in production that had been lacking in the preceeding years.

Although humanitarian problems and the general improvement of the lot of the Soviet citizen were mentioned periodically, the basic thrust of statements on production goals tended to suggest that productivity had become an end in itself. Certainly the goals had gained and were likely to keep high priority for the party elite, who had increasingly tied the party itself to the economic structures and processes of the system and to the premise that party leadership of the economy could stimulate great advances in production.

In addition to maintaining party leadership, increasing productivity, and improving management of the economy, there were of course many more specific objectives. National defense, contrary to our expectations in this study, did not receive any significant emphasis of its own, but was usually treated as a part of maintaining the stability and independence of the system. Furthermore, defense and related strategic matters are rarely discussed before the general Soviet public and therefore do not lend themselves to the type of analysis employed here. Our study must emphasize those goals that the party itself has taken an active and open role in formulating and implementing.

In the material examined some goals were stressed during particular periods and given relatively little attention otherwise. For example, the goal of providing more and better education received three times as many references in 1960 as in the other years examined. The reason for this sharp surge of interest was a school construction program then being pushed very forcefully by the party leadership. Similarly, science and space received greater attention in the years of dramatic accomplishments than in the other years, when the attention given them in *Pravda* was relatively constant. Goals relating to such problems as housing, transportation, and the ethnic minorities received irregular and light attention.

Cultural issues, excluding the minorities problem, received fairly consistent notice in the 1956–1962 period, dropped to a low in 1964, and peaked dramatically in 1966. The increased concern with cultural questions continued into 1968. Most of the references to cultural problems fell under two headings—youth and the literary community. The first concern was sparked primarily by indications of unrest among the youth, especially at some of the institutions of higher education. The Soviet press characterized such youthful dissatisfaction as a product of indifference to socialist values or, in some cases, of excessive independence and personal ambition. The goal of bringing the young intellectuals back into the collective fold was clearly articulated, but the method of doing so was left ambiguous. In general it was proposed to attain the goal through sounder ideological training in socialist morality—as perceived by the party elite. The literary community received much the same sort of attention as did the younger generation, but the people in the two groups only partially overlapped. The party leadership was consistently hostile to underground writers who smuggled their works out of the country for publication abroad. However, the most perplexing problem facing the leadership, one that remained unsolved during the fifteen years after Stalin's death, was that of dealing with the liberal writers who worked within the general boundaries of Soviet legality. The periodic gains and reverses of the liberal literary community reflect the party leadership's indecision as to the proper course of action. *Pravda* editorials seemed to indicate that the post-Khrushchev leadership group were considering or actually planning more conservative and dogmatic goals that would place greater restraints on literary expression.

Particularly striking in our study of goals established by the party is that most of the major and many of the lesser ones have remained relatively constant, but the recommended methods of achieving them and the order of priorities have varied greatly. The controversy over means and priorities may have been more apparent during the Khrushchev years, but surely the whole of the explanation cannot lie in the personal preferences of the First Secretary. Every industrial society has numerous interest aggregations, arising from group functions and other factors. It is to be expected therefore that conflicts will exist in the Soviet hierarchy, that coalitions will shift, and that different priorities will prevail from time to time. Nonetheless, it is impossible to overlook the almost obsessive concern with economic advancement that has dominated the objectives of the Soviet leadership, perhaps since its inception and certainly since the launching of the first five-year plan. The post-Stalin leadership has been more experimental, more concerned with efficiency and broadening the base of the economy, but still has retained its general preoccupation with productivity. What the leadership has apparently just begun to recognize, however, is that the high priority given to economic development and efficiency may pose a serious threat to the kind of political controls that the party has imposed until now. How they will resolve the political-economic controversy is perhaps not so predictable as it would have been under Stalin, so that this remains one of the great questions about the future of the Soviet system.

CHAPTER

5

Goal Attainment

The role of the C.P.S.U. in goal attainment begins with the determination of party members, or more specifically the party elite, to maintain its authoritative position in the Soviet system. Unlike parties in other systems that may expect to be out of power periodically, the C.P.S.U. jealously guards its prerogative to conduct all political recruitment and to control, absorb or eliminate all opposition whether that opposition is present, potential, or imagined. A party out of power may be as anxious as the C.P.S.U. to propagate party goals, but in a party which claims a permanent right to rule, the very propagation of its goals and values has an authority and scope that is uncommon outside of movement-regimes. Similarly, the presumption of permanent rule, reinforced by conviction of the rightness of party goals, influences the party's ways of attaining goals.

Goal attainment in the Soviet system is pursued through extensive preparation of party members and the use of party organs as agencies of supervision and control. In fact, the party's ability to maintain authority and to guide the system toward certain goals is very probably due to its personnel and their placement in strategic positions. The party itself has explained how it exercises leadership of social and governmental organizations: (1) by making certain that the leaders of party organs unswervingly follow the Central Committee; (2) by placing control of all social and governmental organizations under Communists who work in these organizations and through the selection and training of leading cadres; and (3) by exerting influence in non-party organizations through party groups in them.[1] In the official view, therefore, the key to party effectiveness is found in the reliability of its cadres and their strategic placement not only in the party but throughout the socio-political system.

A similar answer was given the question of how the party should implement high-level party decisions. First in importance is "the selection, placement, and education of cadres, the organization of control and examination of performance, and the combination of party-political and party-organizational work with the economy."[2] Second, goal attainment is to be promoted through the "strong observance of Leninist norms of party life and the principle of collective leadership, the promotion among party workers and organs of responsibility of the party masses, and the maintenance of a high level of party activity." Third, the party is to be promoted as "the highest form of social-political organization." Fourth, the unity between the party and the people must be strengthened through cooperation between party and non-party masses. And fifth, further development of internal democracy, criticism, self-criticism of the party, and the strengthening of unity among the party ranks is demanded.

It is obvious from the foregoing that the party considers personnel and structure crucial to its effective operation and maintenance of an essentially monopolistic authority in the system. (The term *monopolistic authority* is not meant to exclude the existence of competing centers of influence; it does, however, mean that group interests must operate through the party structure: there is no other dependable access to the principal decision-makers or to representation in decision-making organs.) Structure is important because it provides channels of communication within the party and state that are essential to the operation of a control system. In other words, structure enables functions to be performed. For this reason, particular attention is given in the following section to structural characteristics of the C.P.S.U., again focusing especially on the Leningrad party organization.

The Relationship of the Party Structure to Economy and Culture

In considering the relationship of party structure and personnel to goal attainment, we will concentrate on the provincial (oblast) and primary party organizations. Although the higher party organs have much greater responsibility in actual decision-making and in coordinating communications, our attention to provincial and lower party organs is justified on two grounds. First, scholars have studied the higher party organs in great detail so that there is already a substantial body of literature on them.[3] Second, considerable power resides in the 137 obkoms and their secretaries; in many respects they are the most important administrative units in the party. The first secretaries of a majority of these provincial party committees are sufficiently important to have membership or candidate membership in the Central Committee. In one sense these secretaries and the apparati over which they preside are the backbone of the party, for they make the decisions of the higher party bodies meaningful by translating them into practical results.

The structure of the Leningrad obkom illustrates both the general organization of the party on the oblast level and the parallels between structure and the socio-economic divisions of the nation. The obkom is headed by a first secretary who has from one to four additional secretaries and a staff of apparatchiki who head and work in the various sections and departments. Party literature suggests that a growing number of these party workers become specialists in different types of party, production, or cultural problems.

1. Department of Party Organs
   a. Section of Statistics and Party Cards
   b. Information Section
   c. Section of Registration of Cadres
2. Department of Propaganda and Agitation
   Press and Lecture Group
3. Department of Culture
4. Department of Science and Middle School Establishments
   Section of Educational Establishments
5. Department of Light and Food Industries and Trade
6. Department of Industry
7. Department of Transport and Communications
8. Department of Construction and City Economy
9. Department of Administrative Organs
10. Department of Agriculture
    Section of Economics
11. *Party-State Control Committee.[4]

The Leningrad obkom has a gorkom and many raikoms working under its general supervision. The Leningrad gorkom has almost the same structure as the obkom. There is a department of organizational party work, with three sections corresponding to the obkom sections. The only differences are that two obkom departments are combined in a single department of science, schools, and culture. A gorkom that embraced an agricultural area would include a department of agriculture, but the Leningrad gorkom has none.

On the raikom level, party activities are commonly assigned to secretaries according to the type of work. In most of the raikoms of the Leningrad oblast, the first secretary is concerned with party organization, the second secretary with industry, transport, and construction, and the third with ideology. The Department of Organization is staffed by a head, a deputy head,

* Party-State Control Committees were subsequently abolished.

and three to nine instructors. The Department of Propaganda and Agitation has a head, a deputy head, and three to five instructors, while the Department of Industry and Transport has two chief administrators and two to four instructors.[5] There are three other sections and formerly there was the Party-State Control Commitee. There is no department of agriculture in most Leningrad raikoms; questions of agriculture are studied by a group of about five persons in the Department of Organization under the direction of the deputy head. In raikoms where agriculture is the principal industry, the first secretary himself is usually an agricultural expert and deals with agricultural problems. In such cases the second secretary is responsible for organizational work and the third with ideological questions.

The structure of a raikom therefore depends on the economy of the region as well as on the size of the population and the number of party organs active in the area. In 1965, the raikom of Smolensk in the Leningrad oblast had three secretaries, three departments, three sections, and the Committee on Party-State Control.[6] The Department of Organization consisted of a head, a deputy head, and nine instructors; the Department of Propaganda and Agitation had a head, a deputy head, five instructors, two lecturers, and one consultant librarian; and the Department of Industry and Transport had a head, a deputy head, and four instructors. In addition, there were Sections of Statistics and Party Cards, Finance, and Economics, each with their directors, and the Committee of Party-State Control headed by a chairman. Thus, the minimum number of persons employed as full-time apparatchiki in the Smolensk raikom was thirty-four and very likely the actual figure was closer to forty. This estimate does not include the first secretaries of primary party organizations located in the raikom.

Pravda reported on January 27, 1962, that there were over 320,000 party workers in the committees of party organizations from the district through the republic levels. Of these, 80,000 were instructors and inspectors, 140,000 were lecturers and speakers, and 105,000 were members of commissions or of party groups in soviets. At all levels of the C.P.S.U. there were 2,110,000 members who served on party committees. The latter figure represented over a fifth of all C.P.S.U. members.

In all there were fifty-two raikom secretaries in the Leningrad oblast in 1965. Virtually all had had at least an incomplete higher education.[7] Forty, or 77 per cent, were specialists in industry. It has also been claimed that "all secretaries of the gorkom and raikoms had experience in party, soviet, and economic work." In addition, 62 per cent of the instructors in the Leningrad obkom and raikoms are considered specialists in either industry or agriculture. All instructors in the branches of departments have "higher engineering–technical education."[8] The emphasis on technically competent cadres in the presentation of this information indicates the priority given by the party leadership to efficiency. It also suggests that the elite feels the need to convince the non-party specialist and worker of the party's ability to provide leadership in the industrial sector.

For the inspectors and supervisors of productive units, technical backgrounds are most important. According to the Party Rules, the party organizations in the oblast are responsible for obtaining adherence to party goals and economic plans. The tasks of the primary party organizations were broadened in 1956–1957, when the political departments and bureaus in the Ministry of Navy, the militia, and the Ministry of Social Security were abolished and their functions transferred to the primary party units.[9] Further changes in the 1961 Party Rules gave the primary organizations powers of inspection in additional enterprises and organizations.[10] Many party cells needed more knowledgeable leadership in order to cope with their extension of authority and thereby increased the demand for cadres with specialized educations.

By 1965, the Leningrad obkom boasted that 72.6 per cent of

the secretaries of the primary party organizations were specialists in either industry or agriculture.[11] There was a total of
6,221 primary units in the oblast although many smaller ones
had no secretaries. Of the total, 2,055 primary units were in
industry, transport, unions, and construction, 147 in state farms,
and 94 on collective farms.[12] The remaining organizations were
in educational, territorial, and military establishments. The principal purpose of the primary organization is clearly stated in
Voprosy partiinoi raboty, an official party sourcebook. "Every-
thing that a primary party organization does is ultimately directed toward the improvement of production figures. . . . Under
every circumstance, the work of a primary party organization
and, as a consequence, of its secretary, is judged by practical
results."[13] This "produce or perish" demand upon the secretary
underscores his need for technical as well as administrative
ability. "The secretary must have knowledge of the industry and
must keep up with developments in similar enterprises. Only by
understanding the technological foundations of the technological processes is he fully qualified to direct the party organization,
to assess accurately the opinions of specialists, and to form his
own opinion in technical matters."[14] With such responsibilities
it is hardly surprising that a large percentage of secretaries are
trained engineers and technicians.

Despite the demands placed on the secretaries of primary
party organizations, their authority has definite limits. Organiza-
tionally, they are under the supervision and directions of secretaries of the raikom and obkom. Furthermore, the local secretary
has no authority over the director of an enterprise, although
the wise director undoubtedly seeks the advice of the secretary
before issuing important orders. Similarly, the secretary has no
official jurisdiction over the hiring and firing of enterprise employees, though once again most managers will confer with him
about important personnel decisions. The two basic prerogatives
of the secretary and the primary party organization are stated in

a party handbook as, (1) the right to inspect the files of an enterprise and to see how its work is progressing, and (2) the right to require regular progress reports from the manager of an enterprise and to make recommendations concerning future work.[15]

Primary party organizations in agricultural enterprises and institutions of higher learning operate in the same general way as those in industrial enterprises. One fundamental difference, however, is the role of the local secretary on collective farms, who is always a member of the management. In addition, he is responsible for inspecting the progress of work on collectives and for maintaining political surveillance of members of the farm. In institutions of higher learning, the primary party secretary and executive committee work closely with the inspector of faculties. Since no actual production is involved, the principal functions of the party are political and usually take the form of persuading faculty and students to behave according to prescribed patterns.

The objective of the party-state is to integrate the party membership with all economic and social sectors in the system and not merely to place party secretaries in strategic positions and assign them control functions. Consequently, the party has sought to develop other forms of leadership to supplement the official executive committees and secretaries. These other forms have involved instructors with the various departments and sections of the oblast, city, and raion party organizations, and also the commissions established by party organizations. The commissions seem increasingly to be used as a principal method of permitting a large number of party activists to participate in productive enterprises and cultural establishments, and to link party activists with non-party activists in such activities.

The structure of commissions is parallel to the primary, raion, and oblast party organizations. They may be organized by the raikom and obkom, but their primary function is to utilize the members of the primary party organization.[16] In the Leningrad oblast in 1965, about 4,000 commissions were operating in production party organizations in which more than 20,000 party members worked. A report on their activities noted, "Commissions remain a major means for strengthening the enterprises of industry, transport, unions, and construction."[17] It is clear that these commissions, though some deal largely with ideological and social questions, are largely production-oriented and that they have essentially an economic purpose.

Commissions are coordinated at the raikom and obkom levels of the party. Available evidence indicates that their core leadership also comes from the raikom and obkom. Their structure and the subjects with which they are concerned may be illustrated by the industrial raikom commissions in Leningrad.

1. Technical-Economic Section
   a. Group for the economic analysis of the use of certain funds
   b. Group for the struggle against waste of working time
2. Section on the Introduction and Distribution of Initiative and Improved Methods of Work
3. Section on Mechanization
   a. Group on the Introduction of Group Processing Details
   b. Group on the Mechanization of Loading and Unloading Work
4. Section on the Introduction of Chemical Materials in the Production of Industrial Enterprises
5. Section on the Mechanization of Engineering and Management
6. Section on Transport
   a. Group on the Safety of Movement
   b. Group on Technical Progress in Transport
7. Section on Construction
8. Council of Innovators[18]

The commissions are intended to facilitate production by providing additional training for party members, managers, and workers who participate in the productive processes. Councils of innovators reward the most innovative participants with in-

creased recognition and status; they also gather the most creative persons for periodic discussions and programs, to stimulate
further creative endeavors.

In the Leningrad oblast in 1965, there were councils of innovators in 265 party organizations with 4,750 people participating.
In addition, 600 party organs had established social construction
bureaus with over 8,000 participants as a means of encouraging
experiments in work techniques and so increasing production
capacity.[19] Almost all raikoms under the Leningrad obkom created cabinets on party construction to prepare members to
work more effectively in commissions and bureaus; the sections
introduced new forms of party organizational work and served
as a permanent consultative organ. In Leningrad in 1964, over
100,000 participated in commissions on assistance to technical
progress, in councils of innovators, in commissions and councils
on ideological work (which are at least partly devoted to practical economics), and in studies of counselling methods for
party-organizational work in industrial enterprises, technical
cabinets, and related organs.[20] The purpose of these organizations was threefold: (1) to reward persons who had shown
initiative, (2) to teach and develop new techniques, and (3) to
promote a sense of collective participation as a means of improving coordination through better official and unofficial communications.

The commission approach is also used in scientific research
institutes and in the party organizations of state institutions.
They parallel the primary party organizations in those bodies.
Their functions are similar to those found in the industrial sector, serving principally as training or educational devices and
as small communications centers within large establishments.

Instructors from the raikom departments are instrumental in
carrying out the work of commissions. Not only do they act as
advisers within commissions but also as communication agents
from commissions to raikom plenums. Furthermore, the raikom

meetings at which they offer their observations and have their questions discussed are relatively open in structure and informative rather than didactic. An official party handbook cautions that discussion should not be confined to "only one secretary of a party organization as had happened in the past" but should include "everyone in the bureau, economists, specialists, and those responsible for that section. . . ."[21] In addition, the handbook recommends that "nonparty specialists, scientific workers, and the best workers in industry" be brought to bureau meetings and committee plenums and encouraged to participate.

Although the party departments of propaganda and agitation regularly promote Marxist-Leninist thought, current Soviet policies, and the ideals of the new Soviet man, most of the work of the other party organizations is practical and involves supervisory and control functions, the expansion of production, and the recruitment of capable and effective party members. The party's role in supervising and expanding production was modified and augmented during the Khrushchev period until it led the list of party priorities. According to *Voprosy partiinogo stroitel'stva,* the party has three principal tasks: (1) the training of cadres for economic construction, (2) the organization of political leadership, and (3) providing the means through which "Marxism-Leninism and Leninist principles of party leadership of economic construction are resolved."[22] The stress is on leadership—economic, political, and ideological—and a major political and ideological purpose of the party is to provide effective organizational leadership in economic development. Its ability to provide leadership is the party's underlying justification for holding supremacy and welds together the party's diversity of organizations and personnel.

The organization and activities of the party obkom and raikom units, the work of commissions, and the work of primary party organizations testify to the party leadership's profound concern for economic functions. This concern is further demonstrated by the fact that stimulating production is a part of the work of the party's propaganda agencies, and by the many conferences, seminars, and lectures conducted by specialists in industry, agriculture, and transportation. A majority of party workers (77 per cent) in 1965 were employed in the sphere of material production.[23] Efforts are also made to get non-party workers to participate in conferences and special work improvement programs. In Leningrad in 1964, 56 per cent of all workers took part in the party movement of Communist work[24] (a leadership program for local party activists to promote the party and its plans). Since 1959, economic conferences and special programs in production have been coordinated by annual conferences in all circles of production in raions, cities, and oblasts.[25] Party directives to local and provincial secretaries urge them to be "party-economic activists" and maintain regular contact with economic leaders.[26] All of the foregoing activities fall under the rubric of "practical party work."

Party Control Functions

Much of the party activity in political socialization and practical economic education can be considered aspects of party control. The surveillance responsibilities of party secretaries also clearly fall into the category of control. For a long period, however, the party leadership was not content to exercise the control function through the normal activities of party organs and party officials, but created an additional formal control mechanism that was at times very powerful. This Party- or Party-State Control Committee existed in one form or another during the post-Stalin period until it was abolished in 1967. The regular party organs then became the principal means of assuring party control in the system.

During their existence, Party–State Control Committees were structured very much like the network of party secretariats. The

Party–State Control Committee of the Central Committee and Council of Ministers operated at the apex of the hierarchical network, with subordinate committees at each lower level of the party organization. The oblast Party–State Control Committees directed the supervisory work of the committees of the raion and primary party organizations. The control functions were exercised basically in economic enterprises, but were also applied in schools and universities.[27] All the Party–State Control Committees were officially under the administration of the plenums of party committees, and their activities never actually replaced the control functions of the obkom, raion, and primary party secretaries or the state procuracy. Rather, the work was done in triplicate without any division of responsibility. It is probable that the gradual development of the Party–State Control Committee system into a miniature bureaucracy with certain resemblances to the old secret police system was a major reason for its abolition. The system was becoming a potential base for aspirants to political power and consequently posed a threat to the secretariat system. In addition, the multiplication of control agencies must have seemed wasteful of human resources to some party leaders and as likely to produce inefficiencies as to promote control.

When the Brezhnev leadership abolished all committees of party-state control, their function devolved primarily upon the regular party organs, especially on their secretaries. The rights of inspection and recommendations were given to the appropriate party organizations to exercise over state enterprises and institutions. At the ministerial level these rights sometimes belong to one of the higher party organs or to the secretariat of the Central Committee itself. A local factory or institution usually is subject to inspection by the primary party organization, which in turn is closely directed by the raikom and obkom. The principal responsibility for seeing that party members carry out their control function belongs to the secretary of the appropriate party organization. Inspection may be accomplished through visits to the organization subject to control and through information gained from organization leaders at party committee sessions, statistical reports, written answers to specific questions, regular written reports to party secretaries, and similar devices.[28]

In addition to exercising its rights to inspect and to recommend, the party directly controls the selection of key personnel, especially at the intermediary and higher levels of the state bureaucracy. This is done through the *nomenklatura,* a list of positions that may be filled only by party members and of party members qualified for each position. In the Leningrad oblast in 1965 about 5,000 people held jobs by virtue of nomenklatura and were officially described as "the primary leadership cadres of the party, soviet, trade union and komsomol organizations who lead industry, construction, agriculture, science, culture, and art."[29] The majority of them have specialized educations and practical experience. There are probably about 200,000 positions in the U.S.S.R. on the nomenklatura.

Since several party members and party organizations may participate in the control functions, coordinating their activities is a major problem. Practically no information is available on informal lines of communication that may facilitate such coordination, but several formal devices used to synchronize methods and aims are known. Purportedly, regular meetings are held in which secretaries and bureau members of raikoms report on their work before secretaries and bureau members of primary party organizations. These meetings are also used to give instructions to the members of primary party organizations. In turn, members from the cells may use these occasions to report on specific problems and to question raikom leaders.[30] Similar conferences are conducted at the obkom level. Despite the inter-level conferences, the principal means of regulating party activities is still the chain of secretariats that link each level of party organization from the primary party unit to the Secretariat of the All–Union Central Committee.

Problems of the Apparatchiki

From the outset of Khrushchev's effort to strengthen the party at the expense of the state bureaucracy, conflict developed not only between apparatchiki and government personnel but within the membership of each. The conflict was generated largely by the open and insistent efforts of the party leadership to impose its views of governmental reform on the state. For example, the lead article in *Kommunist* for November 1956 called for a more efficient state organization and proclaimed that the "party is resolutely struggling to eliminate shortcomings in the government apparatus."[31] The party was clearly insisting on its right to reform the state, which had developed its own institutional standards and interests during the Stalin years. The party's relative bureaucratic inactivity during those years had lulled many government personnel into a sense of security and independence that were now being challenged. The party reasserted its right to regulate forms and to control personnel with an alarming vigor. "Party organizations must see to it that government agencies are headed by capable and tested persons who are devoted to the people and who possess political experience, special qualifications, and organizational abilities."[32] Such a resurgence of party supremacy was unwelcomed in certain circles and was certain to provoke conflict.

Initially the clash was over the division of responsibility between the management of enterprises and the party secretary whose responsibility for increasing efficiency in production inevitably interfered with the prerogatives of management. Party organs were repeatedly instructed to see that all units of the government apparatus were properly organized to carry out their work, but simultaneously cautioned against taking over the functions of government agencies and state enterprises. This was less of a contradiction in orders for the agricultural sector, where the party had long participated in the actual management of collective farms, than it was for the industrial sector, where the traditional apparatchiki had had no opportunity to develop the specialized technical skills possessed by management. The advancement of Soviet industry required an increasing level of specialization among its managers for them to be effective.

Specialization, therefore, once again became a divisive factor among the apparatchiki. Those who were given greater responsibility for the progress of production found it necessary to learn more about the complex mechanics of their field. Their time was allocated more and more to technical matters and less and less to general political matters and theoretical training. Similarly party leadership often became more concerned with the successful organization and direction of various aspects of production than with ideology and non-economic political questions. Specialization, therefore, came to threaten the traditional apparatchiki who were more concerned with political orthodoxy and organizational stability than with initiative, increased efficiency, and quality in production. There is evidence of extreme controversy between these two factions of the apparatus over the party reform of November 1962, which bifurcated the intermediary party organs into industrial and agricultural divisions and in time would have led to two separate sets of apparatchik specialists. It was among the first of Khrushchev's programs to be rejected by his successors in 1964, and it is likely that many economic specialists in the apparatus had serious reservations about the reform from the first. The restoration of the older form of party organization by the Brezhnev-Kosygin leadership, however, has not halted the conflict between those who emphasized the economic responsibility of the party and those who stressed the political tasks.

The post-Khrushchev leadership of the C.P.S.U. attempted to heal the divisions among the apparatchiki by seeking a balance between the economic and political functions of the party. Brezhnev as General Secretary clearly wanted the party to maintain a strong voice in the economic bureaucracy, but he seemed reluctant to follow a course that would transform the party too radically and abruptly. The party had to provide economic leadership but it also had to maintain a measure of political independence from the economic structures. Otherwise the party might eventually be absorbed into the state bureaucracy. Already some functionaries seemed to fear that it had begun to move in that direction.

The problem of orientation and role specialization was unexpectedly aired in a series of articles and letters printed in *Partinaia zhizn'* in 1965. All the contributors took up some aspect of the generalist versus specialist or the political orientation versus economic orientation controversy. Moreover, different views of the problem clearly showed through the moderate positions most frequently espoused.

One author bemoaned the preference given to industrial or agricultural specialists when personnel was recruited for the party apparatus. "To some extent this is justified," he admitted, for "the specialist knows production and technology, and that is good."[33] But, he complained, "it is bad when insufficient attention is paid to whether the specialist has a natural inclination for party work, whether he understands its distinctive features and is suited to it by character." The writer then observed that experience had "frequently" disproved the belief that the specialist would acquire an understanding of party work. "Even now," he said, "one meets people in the party apparatus who may understand production and technology quite well but who cannot analyze the work of a party unit, generalize experience, carry through the proposals made by Communists and workers, or perceive the mood of masses. . . ." A good party functionary must display "broad knowledge, a creative attitude, and a constant search for the new," he asserted. "Poorly prepared people with inadequate political and specialized knowledge get into the party apparatus" and lower the quality of its work. Here was the voice of a generalist, though not necessarily an ideologue, who felt threatened by specialization and what he assumed to be favoritism in the apparatus toward the specialist.

Another critic of the specialist complained that "an excessive interest on the part of party agencies in purely economic and narrowly practical matters has led to a slackening of attention to internal party life and has had a negative effect on the basic links of organizational work, such as work with cadres and checking on how resolutions are implemented."[34] The writer was alarmed because in the last three years "nearly all the secretaries and bureau members" had been replaced by specialists. "A one-sided approach to the recruitment of cadres, with a strong inclination toward direct intervention in the economy, is especially apparent when we examine the composition of the membership of party bureaus, party committees, and secretaries of the primary party units." While concurring with efforts to bring forward fresh minds, this writer was disturbed because in recent years advancements in the apparatus had gone mainly to specialists from various fields of the economy. Recruiting and promoting party apparatchiki had become in his estimation a "mechanical" process too much linked with "possession of a diploma." He urged greater heed to the individual's "political qualities or organizational abilities." This apparatchik clearly sensed a difference in the character of new personnel and felt that the specialization of the newcomer threatened the political life of the party as he had known it.

In opposition to the articles noted above, delegates to a party conference responded by insisting that "there should be no tolerance of instances in which the apparatus works for its own sake, forgetting that its chief purpose is to help the primary organizations and to guide Communists toward the accomplishment of vital tasks."[35] To them "vital tasks" were primarily productive tasks. They saw the educational function of the party and the effort to mold the new Communist man as essentially a means of creating achievement-oriented, production-conscious individuals better able to facilitate the economic development of the system. Another writer argued more objectively that duplication of the work of managerial officials by party leaders was unavoidable as long as the party's organizational work concentrated on productive units of society. The problem therefore was the lack of a firm decision as to what responsibility the party should have in the field of production.[36]

This controversy reveals the close relationship of the recruitment function and the goal attainment function. The more responsibility the party assumes in technical matters, the greater is its need for specialists. The party's direct involvement in the exceedingly complex and rapidly changing system of production has made inevitable the rise of the specialist in the party apparatus. Even if the increasing influence of the specialist should somehow be confined to an official advisory role, the authority of the generalist would still be limited by the technical nature of the advice required.

The party has transformed itself by recruiting only the elite of Soviet society and by assuming a responsibility for the operation of the economic bureaucracy. In the future the party may be less and less successful in differentiating between itself and the state and in placing the burden of failures on a bureaucracy for which it has assumed final responsibility.

In general the party may be said to have recourse to three procedures for attaining specified objectives. One of these is normative, the prescribing of authoritative standards; this is made possible by the strategic placement of personnel and by the participation of party personnel in making and reviewing decisions. Normative means are further applied through the socialization process that prescribes standards for individual and collective relationships and influences the ordinary behavior patterns of men and of groups. The numerous lectures, seminars, and commissions are among the more obvious means employed by the party to foster normative standards and thereby to influence behavior. A second means of goal attainment is coersion. Party influence over non-party personnel, threats of bad reports to superiors, criminal penalties for violations of official rules, and many ways of imposing personal liability all give the party an effective coercive force. And, finally, a system of rewards provides a positive means for the party to encourage behavior conducive to the attainment of its goals. Promotions, awards and honors, special privileges, and financial incentives are used to engender competition when it is deemed desirable for the advancement of party objectives. All of these means operate effectively because of the advantages afforded by the party structure, with its tight lines of command and competent intra-party communications system. Although the latter is effective in carrying communications from the top of the hierarchy to the bottom, however, the party may increasingly feel the need for a more competent flow of communications in the opposite direction. To what degree the present structure and procedures at the lower levels of the Soviet party system can provide that competence may be seriously questioned.

6

Conclusion

Examination of the functions of political socialization, recruitment, goal specification and goal attainment raises questions as to appropriate conceptual approaches both for the study of the Soviet system and for comparative political analysis in general. On the negative side it must be recognized that the four functions do not in themselves cover all possible categories; they overlap each other and there is no absolute delineation between them. This difficulty, however, is not necessarily inherent in our functional model. Rather, the problem results largely from the involvement of so many of the same personnel in all major functions of the Soviet system (and others as well). The functional analyst thus is called upon to distinguish between different roles performed by the same persons. This is a difficult task in any system, for role function analysis requires psychological research and long-term observations of behavior offered to social scientists by few political systems. Among the problems in properly defining functions, the most critical is that of consistently discerning the different role functions performed by each individual in view of the influence that the norms and values of each role have on other roles.

On the positive side, functional examination of the C.P.S.U. does provide a useful means of studying and evaluating the political integration of the Soviet system. Because the principal functions of the party all come together in promoting integration, this is a particularly fruitful approach. In addition, factors militating against integration may be discerned more clearly than in many alternative modes of analysis. Since integration is particularly important to developing systems, whether Communist or non-Communist, functional analysis may prove especially fruitful in studies of developing nations. Among developing countries, those properly characterized as mass movement–regimes may yield to the functional approach most successfully. Of course, only time and effort can determine that.

Among the integrative functions are goal specification and goal attainment, which are dependent upon each other but distinctive in their individual attributes. The characteristics of the goal functions are largely determined by the processes of political recruitment and political socialization, and those have therefore been given primary attention for the purposes of this analysis.

Recruitment by the C.P.S.U. is primarily a leadership function that brings into the party the personnel necessary to provide control and representation. Control is largely accomplished through supervisory and administrative agencies but is supplemented by the extensive political education program described in our discussion of the political socialization function. Representation of various groups in the Soviet party system is provided by co-optation, which insures that key leadership groups work through the party mechanism from the local to the national levels. The party aim in recruitment is abetted by the upward mobility that aspiring citizens often enjoy from membership in the C.P.S.U.

Recruitment in many respects is the key to the success of the C.P.S.U. in maintaining its vital role in furthering the stability of the system. It is also a continuing problem that could result either in the gradual erosion of the party's monopolistic position in the system or its eventual transformation into a very different type of organization from what it was during the 1950's and

1960's. The future characteristics of the C.P.S.U. will probably be determined in large measure by the kinds of individuals recruited during the Khrushchev and Brezhnev years and by the intra-party and party/non-party channels of communication that develop as these new recruits move up in the party hierarchy. The goal functions and socialization process should be influenced considerably by previous recruitment patterns.

Since the Bolsheviks took power in 1917, the party leadership has recognized the importance of recruitment and has been alert to the difficulties that certain kinds of recruitment could bring to the system. During both the Lenin and Stalin eras the party alternated between rapid growth and mass expulsions. Opportunists who had joined the party from expediency rather than commitment were ferreted out, especially during the early years of Bolshevik rule. Members who were thought rightly or wrongly to have associated with ideological dissidents within the party usually met with the same fate. Over one million party members were dismissed in the great purges of 1936–1938, many of whom had been among the earliest members of the C.P.S.U. The 1930's also witnessed the beginnings of massive recruitment of members for their administrative and technical skills. As an increasingly complex Soviet society needed more and more professional specialization to achieve administrative and economic progress, the party leadership sought to recruit members for their leadership potential in key sectors of the burgeoning socio-economic system. Since Stalin, the party has undertaken recruitment drives specifically to attract specialists with needed education and experience, but at this time of writing, it has mounted no expulsion campaign in any way comparable with the upheavals in membership that occurred between 1918 and 1952. This change may be attributed partly to the leadership's concern for the stability of the regime, but an even more compelling reason has been the growing and necessary reliance on specialists in numerous fields. Such people are often not easily replaced, especially when about two-thirds of those with completed higher educations are already members of the party. Scarcity of supply undoubtedly has something to do with the party elite's reluctance or inability to purge opportunists who have little or no ideological commitment and seek to advance themselves solely on the basis of their professional expertise.

It is reasonable to assume that keeping up with the technical knowledge needed for supervising modern industry and production will eventually, indeed if it is not already doing so, further limit the party's freedom of choice in selecting new members. Even now the demand for party leaders and cadres with an economic orientation is changing the character of the apparatchiki. Certainly if efficiency and success in production become the principal criteria for rewarding party functionaries as they have for managers of enterprises, the long-range effect on both the values and norms of the system may be even more dramatic than the ideological erosion already evident. The party is clearly in a dilemma of major importance. In order to strengthen its control of the economic bureaucracy, the party leadership has demanded greater economic and technical preparation of its own personnel. This very choice suggests that the party leadership found political and ideological controls inadequate and sought to supplement them by extending party responsibility for economic development. Yet their very choice may well have begun to undermine the character of the party by changing the standards of leadership and the criteria for evaluating its work. Soon, the loyalty and ideological purity still demanded of Soviet citizens may come to be demonstrated by contributions to the material advance of the economy, through making successful innovations, and by showing professional and technical competence.

The Brezhnev leadership of the party has shown itself aware of the dilemma. On the one hand it has prepared the party to continue its supervision of the economy by pursuing the Khrushchev policies of recruitment and promotion of cadre specialists to better party posts. On the other hand, the leadership has been hypersensitive to intellectual ferment in the U.S.S.R. and in other party-states and has sought to strengthen the party's social control by pursuing its programs of political socialization with renewed vigor.

The urgent concern of the party elite with formal programs of political socialization indicates both lack of confidence in winning spontaneous support and the desire to impose a total value system on Soviet citizens. From the outset of the Soviet system, the party has used propaganda and agitation in the attempt to bring about common basic behavior patterns and value orientations, and so to achieve social and political integration. During the post-Stalin period, Soviet political socialization has developed into a curious blend of didactic techniques and practical education, but whatever the approach, the process has been aimed at achieving integration and certain specific goals.

The didactic approach to political socialization was foreshadowed in Bolshevik propaganda prior to the 1917 revolution. The attainment of power, of course, brought the means to disseminate propaganda officially and on a large scale. Propaganda campaign techniques have changed to some extent with technological developments, but the general approach has remained remarkably the same. Confidence has persisted that short dogmatic statements militantly presented will influence the attitudes and behavior of listeners, readers, and viewers. This confidence has issued in an invariable didactic approach to agitation-propaganda wherever used—in the school system and youth organizations, in the press, and in posters, radio, television, and public speeches. All these techniques have been used from the beginning to cultivate the new Soviet man, the typical citizen dedicated to the collective achievement of the nation, whose total behavior and thought is directed to the fulfillment of that end.

As the economic successes of the system have whetted the

Soviet appetite for greater and more rapid material achievements, the political socialization processes have increasingly turned to promoting "practical" education that is almost entirely achievement-oriented. This is a major indication of the impact of technological development on the system. The complexities that automation and other technological advances have introduced into modern work patterns have made it necessary to reeducate many already in the labor force and to require greater specialization for the future among Soviet workers, educators, managers, and party cadres. As is often the case, the introduction of the new provoked some difficulties with the old. The expanded use of industrial propaganda has necessitated the reeducation of many cadres already working in the party apparatus and the recruitment of new cadres with specialized education and experience. Apparently the party leadership believed that the need was pressing, for during the decade after 1955 there was a seemingly urgent recruitment campaign and many party functionaries were replaced by others who better met the new specifications.

The growth of practical education was bitterly resisted by those who were more attuned to the traditional political and ideological emphasis in party propaganda. There was never any question, of course, of abandoning political-ideological agitation and propaganda; rather, it was a matter of giving more attention to economic education and to the recruitment and promotion of the new generation of party functionaries. Nevertheless, the misgivings of the old guard cadres were quite real.

Intellectual ferment among intellectuals in the Soviet Union and in other Communist states did far more than the complaints of the old style cadres to renew the Brezhnev leadership's concern for the political-ideological tasks of the party. Pressure to conform to established norms could still be exerted by party agents and instruments. Agitation for democratization in Czechoslovakia and for freedom of expression in the U.S.S.R. aroused dark suspicions about the political reliability of the populace, or at least of certain segments of the intelligentsia. These fears led the party leaders to renewed use of one of the traditional Soviet means of combatting dissent—stepped up political propaganda campaigns. Failure of these campaigns to achieve the desired results may sometimes cause them to be reinforced by legal and police measures against selected dissidents in the U.S.S.R. In the case of Czechoslovakia, military control was imposed as a last resort after the propaganda campaign waged from Moscow had failed to restrain the reform activities of the Czechoslovak political leaders.

The revival of political education, however, remained secondary to the continuing emphasis on "practical" education. The high priority given to material growth would probably assure the continued prominence of economic education unless, as now seems unlikely, a strong wave of political discontent should sweep the country. More probably, the party elite would continue to stress practical propaganda in an attempt to promote advances in production while employing political propaganda to promote political stability and motivate workers in their efforts to increase output. In any event, there is little prospect that material progress will lead to the political or social liberalization of the regime. Recent trends have given no indication that the technocrats now rising in the C.P.S.U. have any natural inclination to reduce restrictions on speech, press, and assembly. Indeed, should the efficiency-minded engineers presently assuming strategic posts in the party conclude that independent expression is disruptive and liable to hinder economic and social progress, there is no reason to suppose that they would hesitate to impose rigid regulations to curb it. What is more, the greater the leaders' success in fostering economic progress, the more effective they may be in enforcing strong social controls by political or even military means, for the hope of achieving material satisfaction may, at least in the short run, disarm public sympathy with those who criticize the system from a non-material viewpoint.

The drive to develop a highly efficient process of goal specification may in one way run counter to the maintenance of a permanent and rigid system of expression control. That is, effective long-range decision-making requires not only the ability to enforce decisions but assurance that the decisions made are operationally sound and will lead to the desired results. This ability in turn depends in large measure on the efficiency of the information flow available to the decision-makers. The growing complexities of modern society are likely to require a growing communications network among those responsible for making decisions, specialists in the fields involved in particular decisions, those responsible for implementing decisions, and those most affected by the decisions. This demands an expansion of the communications system so that decision-makers may be better able to make sound policy judgments. A necessary corollary is the enlargement of communications channels to the centers of authority, which implies a broadening of representative or quasi-representative forms and a relaxation of controls over the communications network. Such a need, of course, works for divergent forms of expression and organization and against a long-term program of repression.

As long as efficiency remains a fundamental objective of the party leadership and influences the choice of goals, the requirements of goal specification may encourage some relaxation of controls. However, the tendency of the leaders to implement goals through mass mobilization techniques may be expected to restrain any extended relaxation. Furthermore, any development that seems to threaten the system will surely make the goal of protecting the system the primary one, overriding any relaxations of control that may be in effect.

The drive for increased efficiency and productivity dates back to the initiation of the N.E.P. in 1921, but it has gradually become more sophisticated as time has passed. During the post-Stalin period, a new generation of technically proficient, administratively adept party leaders has come into power. Until the late 1950's and early 1960's, their advent was most apparent at the top of the hierarchy. Then such well-trained technocrats began to move into provincial and lower party posts on a large scale. As this movement has continued, the character of party cadres and leaders has begun to change from that of the traditional types. Despite efforts to retard the cadre's transformation into a group of economic and managerial specialists, the shifting requirements for membership in the party elite worked against the old guard. In the first place, the leadership of the Secretariat sought to make the party an effective instrument of control over the bureaucracy, especially over its economic substructures. In the second place, the party leaders' desire to make more effective operational decisions required institutionalizing the input and feedback channels, a move achieved through the membership of the Central Committee and the uses of that body. Both developments increased the party's tendency to recruit or co-opt vast numbers of actual and potential leaders into the C.P.S.U. at every organizational level of the system.

The communications patterns and recruitment policies that have emerged from the party's efforts to integrate the components of the system and to advance goals of efficiency and productivity are closely associated with the questions of how authoritarian is the C.P.S.U. and how accurate it is to characterize the system as totalitarian. Probably most Sovietologists agree that there have been periods in which the leaders of the party appeared unconstrained by social and economic pressures and in which they sought to prevent the development of distinct channels of feedback information outside the control of the party elite. It is highly questionable, however, whether a situation can long endure in which the leadership simply dispenses decisions and then closes all doors. Certainly, it is profoundly questionable whether a leadership that seeks to promote efficient political and economic administration, rational planning, and thorough social integration can maintain its position without permitting the development of a communications network so that the leaders can make the most informed decisions possible. This, in turn, requires meaningful feedback to the decision-makers and increased accessibility of the leadership. Accessibility may be achieved through different structures in different systems. In the U.S.S.R. it appears to be provided largely through recruitment practices that assure the party of ready communications with appropriate specialists, group elites, and supervisory personnel. The long-term development of a rational practice of co-optation, however, has not only assured the party of regular access to important sections of the system but has begun to have the effect of integrating the party into the socio-economic structure. As specialized roles become more and more crucial in the increasingly complex system, the present generation of C.P.S.U. recruits may bring about some fundamental changes in the party's characteristics. Even now, developments in communications and recruitment have seriously restricted the party's freedom of action and made it impossible to isolate the C.P.S.U. from the influence of Soviet socio-economic institutions.

For the same reasons, the totalitarian label as applied to the Soviet system is open to serious challenge unless that concept is drastically redefined. Decision-making in an advanced or rapidly developing system requires a broadening communications network. Furthermore, role specialization accelerates development of subsystems that tend to restrain the central decision-making bodies. There is no evidence yet that these subsystems have become autonomous (that is, able to organize and pursue goals freely according to their special functions and concerns in society), but several of them have achieved semi-autonomous status in the Soviet system through the professionalization of their members. Professionalization makes it difficult for the party elite to replace large numbers of specialists at will. Individuals in key subsystems such as the military may be replaced, and so, perhaps, can sizable numbers of people in less crucial subsystems. But over a gradually but constantly widening range of functional groups and their elites, mass purges and terror are becoming increasingly impractical methods of control. In short, the very goals of the party elite regarding more efficient production, management, and economic planning work against the indiscriminate use of power. This is not to say that the leadership has abandoned its concern for the values and behavior of the total society: rather, our contention is that the party has not discovered how to attain such control without disrupting the integrative processes and goals that it has come to sponsor. Where practical goals of social and economic achievement are deemed more important than control of the social system at any cost, procedural restraints have probably so developed that the indiscriminate use of power is no longer a live option for the leaders of the regime. This does not necessarily apply to Soviet actions in the countries under its sphere of influence, although it is too soon to know what, if any, lessons the leadership of the U.S.S.R. may have learned in the aftermath of the August 1968 invasion of Czechoslovakia. Even that drastic use of force was not unrestrained.

Perhaps what emerges most clearly from a functional analysis of the C.P.S.U. is that the party is the dominant instrument of integration in the system and that this integrative role has begun to have a reverse influence on the character of the party itself. This suggests that in the long run the party cannot be only the integrator but must learn to bend to the economic and social demands and needs of the subjects of the integrative process. The study further suggests that examination of functional roles and processes of a political system may lead to fruitful comparisons of different systems, especially of those characterized by mass movements or dominant parties. In these systems, the conscious use of political means to foster integration of the system often results in blurred distinctions between ostensibly separate organizations, such as party and legislature. Consequently, the functions performed by mass movements and their relationships to governmental organs and to economic and social subsystems may be identified more comprehensively through functional classification, description, and analysis.

NOTES

1. Functional Analysis of Political Parties

1. Robert C. Tucker, "Towards a Comparative Politics of Movement-Regimes," *The American Political Science Review*, Vol. LV, No. 2 (June, 1961), pp. 281–289.

2. See Adam Bromke, ed., *The Communist States at the Crossroads*, New York: Praeger, 1965; J. F. Brown, *The New Eastern Europe*, New York: Praeger, 1966; Stephen Fischer-Galati, ed., *Eastern Europe in the Sixties*, New York: Praeger, 1963; Richard Lowenthal, *World Communism*, New York: Oxford University Press, 1964; Alvin Z. Rubenstein, *Communist Political Systems*, Englewood Cliffs, N.J.: Prentice-Hall, 1966; H. Gordon Skilling, *The Governments of Communist East Europe*, New York: Thomas Y. Crowell, 1966.

3. Walter Buckley, *Sociology and Modern Systems Theory*, Englewood Cliffs, N.J.: Prentice-Hall, 1967, p. 32.

4. Karl W. Deutsch, *The Nerves of Government*, The Free Press of Glencoe, 1963, p. 88.

5. Karl W. Deutsch, "Mechanism, Teleology, and Mind," *Philosophy and Phenomenological Research*, 12 (1951), pp. 200–201.

6. Ibid., p. 201.

7. Gregory Bateson, *Naven*, Cambridge, Mass.: Oxford University Press, 1936, p. 29.

8. P. A. Sorokin, *Social and Cultural Dynamics*, Totowa, N.J.: Bedminster Press, 1937–41, Vol. I, pp. 15, 23. Also see Don Martindale, *Institutions, Organizations and Mass Society*, Boston: Houghton Mifflin, 1966, pp. 32–42.

9. Robert Merton, *Social Theory and Social Structure*, The Free Press of Glencoe, 1957, pp. 49–55.

10. Ibid., pp. 50–51.

11. See Talcott Parsons, *The Social System*, The Free Press of Glencoe, 1951, and *Structure and Process in Modern Societies*, The

Free Press of Glencoe, 1960. For an examination of Parsons' concepts of politics, see William C. Mitchell, *Sociological Analysis and Politics: The Theories of Talcott Parsons*, Englewood Cliffs, N.J.: Prentice-Hall, 1967.

12. William C. Mitchell, *The American Polity*, The Free Press of Glencoe, 1962. Chaps. 13–14.

13. Karl W. Deutsch, "Integration and the Social System," *The Integration of Political Communities*, edited by Philip E. Jacob and James V. Toscano, Philadelphia: Lippincott, pp. 179–186.

14. Sigmund Neumann, "Toward a Comparative Study of Political Parties," *Modern Political Parties*, Chicago: University of Chicago Press, 1956, pp. 395–421.

15. Gabriel A. Almond and G. Bingham Powell, Jr., *Comparative Politics: A Developmental Approach*, Boston: Little, Brown, 1966. See pp. 103–126.

16. Ibid., p. 125.

17. David E. Apter, "Introduction," *Comparative Politics: A Reader*, edited by Harry Eckstein and David E. Apter, The Free Press of Glencoe, 1963, pp. 327–331.

18. Neumann, op. cit., p. 400.

19. Deutsch, *The Nerves of Government*, title and theme of the concluding chapter.

2. Political Recruitment

1. The data contained in the tables on general party membership are found in *Partiinaia zhizn'* 1 (January, 1962), pp. 44–54 and *Partiinaia zhizn'* 10 (May, 1965), pp. 8–17.

2. *Pravda*, March 30, 1966.

3. This figure is based on estimates derived from Nicholas De-Witt, *Educational and Professional Employment in the U.S.S.R.*, Washington, D.C.: Government Printing Office, 1961. A similar estimate is found in Zbigniew Brzezinski and Samuel P. Huntington, *Political Power: U.S.A./U.S.S.R.*, New York: The Viking Press, 1964, p. 168.

4. *Partiinaia zhizn'* 1 (January, 1962), p. 48.

5. The most accessible source of biographical data is *Who's Who in the U.S.S.R., 1965–1966*, compiled by the Institute for the Study of the U.S.S.R, Munich, Germany, and published by the Scarecrow Press, Inc., 1966. Additional information is available in the files of the

Institute. Short but current biographical sketches are published in the *Ezhegodnik* of the *Great Soviet Encyclopedia.* More extensive biographies, though sometimes less up-to-date, are found in *Biograficheskii slovar'*, produced at different times by different professional groups (scientists, engineers, etc.) in the U.S.S.R.

6. References to the background characteristics of the Central Committee membership between 1961 and 1966 are based on Michael P. Gehlen, "The Educational Backgrounds and Career Orientations of the Members of the Central Committee of the C.P.S.U.," *The American Behavioral Scientist*, Vol. IX, No. 8 (April, 1966), pp. 11–14.

7. Principal works dealing with the politics of the Politburo and Secretariat in the post-Stalin period are Brzezinski and Huntington, op. cit.; Robert Conquest, *Power and Policy in the U.S.S.R.*, New York: St. Martin's Press, 1961; Wolfgang Leonhard, *The Kremlin since Stalin*, New York: Praeger, 1963; Roger Pethybridge, *A Key to Soviet Politics*, New York: Praeger, 1962; and Sidney I. Ploss, *Conflict and Decision-Making in the U.S.S.R.*, Princeton: Princeton University Press, 1965.

8. *Staffing Procedures and Problems in the Soviet Union*, a study prepared for the U. S. Senate Committee on Government Operations, Washington, D.C.: Government Printing Office, 1963, p. 9.

9. Ibid., p. 14.

10. DeWitt, op. cit.

11. *Stenograficheskii otchet*, Plenums of the Central Committee of the C.P.S.U. (June, 1963, March, 1964, March, 1965), Moscow: Izdatel'stvo Politicheskoi Literatury, 1963, 1964, 1965.

12. See Philip Selznick, *TVA and the Grassroots*, University of California Publications in Culture and Society (no date), Vol. III, pp. 259–261.

3. The Role of the C.P.S.U. in Political Socialization

1. *Voprosy partiinogo stroitel'stva*, Leningrad Higher Party School, Lenizdat, 1965, p. 370.

2. *Ideologicheskaia rabota partiinykh organizatsii*, Izdatel'stvo of the Higher Party School and Academy of Sciences, prepared for the Central Committee of the C.P.S.U., Moscow, 1963, pp. 7 and 10.

3. *Voprosy partiinogo stroitel'stva*, p. 277.

4. *Ideologicheskaia rabota . . .* , p. 5.

5. Ibid., p. 6.

6. *Voprosy partiinogo stroitel'stva*, p. 333.

7. Ibid., pp. 316–318.

8. *Ideologicheskaia rabota* . . . , p. 28.

9. See *Pravda*, August 10, 1956.

10. *Voprosy partiinogo stroitel'stva*, p. 319.

11. *Ideologicheskaia rabota* . . . , p. 28.

12. *Pravda*, August 30, 1956.

13. *Ideologicheskaia rabota*, p. 14.

14. Ibid., p. 31.

15. Ibid., pp. 19–20.

16. *Spravochnik partiinogo rabotnika*, 3, 1961, p. 456.

17. *Voprosy partiinoi raboty*, Gosudarstvennoe izdatel'stvo politicheskoi literatury, Moscow, 1959, p. 217.

18. Ibid., p. 222.

19. Ibid., pp. 224–225.

20. Ibid., p. 225. Also see the documentary account of the responsibilities of primary party organizations in *Spravochnik sekretaria pervichnoi organizatsii*, Gosdarstvennoe izdatel'stvo politicheskoi literatury, Moscow, 1960.

21. *Voprosy partiinogo stroitel'stva*, p. 37.

22. Ibid., p. 239.

23. Ibid., pp. 308–309.

24. Ibid., p. 282.

25. Ibid., pp. 280–281.

26. Ibid., p. 312.

27. Ibid., pp. 313–314.

28. Ibid., p. 302.

29. Ibid., p. 309.

30. Ibid., p. 307. *Pravda*, May 15, 1957, noted that in the city of Minsk there were reported 1,000 schools, circles and seminars, including 12 economic schools, about 500 economic circles and seminars and 194 circles and seminars on current politics. "The circles, seminars and schools are led by 446 industrial specialists, 26 agricultural specialists, 155 economic workers and more than 300 scientists. There are 21 seminars on the economics of construction, 25 on the economics of trade, 6 on the economics of transportation as well as seminars on the economics of the lumber industry, finance and other areas." From this and similar reports it can be assumed that many of the political-economic education courses are highly specialized and utilitarian in orientation.

31. Ibid., pp. 313–314.

32. *Kommunist*, No. 14, 1962, p. 55.

33. *Pravda*, January 13, 1965. Also see *Partiia i massy*, Academy of Social Science, prepared for the Central Committee of the C.P.S.U., Izdatel'stvo mysl', Moscow, 1966, pp. 100–101 and *Partiinaia zhizn'*, No. 20, 1967, p. 11.

34. *Partiinaia zhizn'*, No. 6, 1956, pp. 3–10.

35. *Voprosy ideologicheskoi raboty partii*, Academy of Social Sciences, prepared for the Central Committee of the C.P.S.U., Izdatel'stvo mysl', Moscow, 1966, p. 9.

36. Ibid., p. 20.

37. Ibid., pp. 22–24.

38. *Voprosy partiinogo stroitel'stva*, p. 380.

39. See Frederick C. Barghoorn, *Politics in the U.S.S.R.*, Boston: Little, Brown, 1966, especially chapters III, IV, and V. Also note Jeremy R. Azrael, "Soviet Union," Chapter 8 of *Education and Political Development*, edited by James S. Coleman, Princeton: Princeton University Press, 1965.

40. *Spravochnik partiinogo rabotniki*, 4, Gosudarstvennoe izdatel'stvo, Moscow, 1963, pp. 428–429.

41. *Voprosy partiinogo stroitel'stva*, p. 394.

42. Ibid., p. 393.

43. Ibid., p. 315.

44. *Partiia i massy*, p. 108. Also see *Itogi vyborov i sostav deputatov Verkhovnykh Sovetov soiuznykh, avtonomykh respublik i mestnykh Sovetov trudiashchiskaia 1963*, Statisticheskii sbornik, pp. 184–185.

45. *K.P.S.S. i massovye organizatsii trudiashchikhsia*, Academy of Social Sciences, Izdatel'stva Higher Party School, Moscow, 1963, p. 28.

46. Ibid.

47. Ibid., p. 30.

48. *Voprosy partiinogo stroitel'stva*, p. 14.

49. *Komsomolskaia pravda*, February 28, 1957.

50. *Voprosy partiinogo stroitel'stva*, p. 96.

51. Ibid.

52. *Pravda*, May 17, 1957.

53. Allen Kassof, *The Soviet Youth Program*, Cambridge, Mass.: Harvard University Press, 1965, p. 77.

54. *Kommunist*, No. 10, 1965, p. 3.

55. *Voprosy partiinogo stroitel'stva*, p. 560.

56. Ibid., p. 576.
57. Ibid., p. 108.
58. *K.P.S.S. i massovye* . . . , pp. 47–50.
59. *Partiinaia zhizn'*, No. 22, 1956, pp. 3–8.
60. See *Pravda*, January 5, 1957.
61. See *Pravda*, December 27, 1956.

4. The C.P.S.U. and Goal Specification

1. See John A. Armstrong, *The Politics of Totalitarianism,* New York: Random House, 1961; Robert Conquest, *Power and Policy in the U.S.S.R.,* New York: St. Martin's Press, 1961; Roger Pethybridge, *A Key to Soviet Politics,* New York: Praeger, 1962; Myron Rush, *The Rise of Khrushchev,* Washington, D.C.: Public Affairs Press, 1958; Robert C. Tucker, *The Soviet Political Mind,* New York: Praeger, 1963.
2. Carl Linden, *Khrushchev and the Soviet Leadership, 1957–1964,* Baltimore: Johns Hopkins Press, 1966.
3. *Staffing Procedures and Problems in the Soviet Union,* U.S. Senate Committee on Government Operations, 88th Congress, Washington, D.C.: Government Printing Office, 1963, p. 24.
4. See *Pravda*, August 14, 1958, September 1, 1958, and December 1, 1958.
5. *Pravda*, December 25, 1958.
6. *Pravda*, January 15, 1962.
7. *Pravda*, May 10, 1962.
8. *Pravda*, February 21, 1966.

5. Goal Attainment

1. *Voprosy partiinogo stroitel'stva,* p. 18.
2. Ibid., p. 34.
3. See Merle Fainsod, *How Russia Is Ruled,* rev. ed., Cambridge, Mass.: Harvard University Press, 1963, and Leonard Schapiro, *The Communist Party of the Soviet Union,* New York: Random House, 1960.
4. *Voprosy partiinogo stroitel'stva,* p. 184.
5. Ibid., pp. 185–186.
6. Ibid., p. 185.
7. Ibid., p. 224.
8. Ibid., p. 224.

9. See *Partiia i massy,* p. 94 and *Spravochnik partiinogo rabotnika,* Gospolitizdat 1957, pp. 405–409, 429, and 436–437.

10. See Article 59 of the Party Statutes.

11. *Voprosy partiinogo stroitel'stva,* p. 224.

12. Ibid., p. 200.

13. Ibid., p. 313.

14. Ibid., pp. 228–229.

15. *Voprosy partiinogo rabotnika,* pp. 237–238.

16. *Voprosy partinogo stroitel'stva,* p. 197.

17. Ibid., pp. 197–198.

18. Ibid., p. 476.

19. Ibid., p. 210.

20. Ibid., pp. 268–269.

21. Ibid., p. 187.

22. Ibid., p. 429.

23. *Partiinaia zhizn',* No. 10 (May, 1965), p. 14.

24. *Voprosy partiinogo stroitel'stva,* p. 437.

25. *Voprosy ideologicheskoi raboty partii,* p. 42.

26. *Voprosy partiinogo stroitel'stva,* p. 226.

27. Ibid., p. 595.

28. Ibid., pp. 253–254.

29. Ibid., p. 223.

30. Ibid., p. 270.

31. *Kommunist,* No. 17 (November, 1956), pp. 3–16.

32. Ibid.

33. *Partiinaia zhizn',* No. 12 (June, 1965), pp. 33–37.

34. *Partiinaia zhizn',* No. 16 (August, 1965), pp. 33–39.

35. *Partiinaia zhizn',* No. 19 (October, 1965), pp. 50–59.

36. *Partiinaia zhizn',* No. 22 (November, 1965), pp. 38–41.

Index

Academy of Sciences, 38, 77; president of, 62

Academy of Social Sciences, 29, 73, 76, 87; president of, 63

Agitprop, 75, 76

Almond, Gabriel, 4, 6, 11; Almond and Powell, 11–12

Apter, David, 11, 12

Armstrong, John, 4

Barghoorn, Frederick C., 89

Bateson, Gregory, 7

Brezhnev-Kosygin (regime), 113, 114, 134

Brezhnev, Leonid, attack on Party-State Control Commission, 131; industrial propaganda, 88; leadership of the Central Committee, 60, 63–65; and the Presidium of the Supreme Soviet, 57; report to the 23rd Congress, 36, 109, 110, 113; as General Secretary, 56, 135, 143

Buckley, William, 5

Central Auditing Commission, 61

Central Committee of the C.P.S.U., plenums, 60–66; propaganda, 76, 78

Communist Party of the Soviet Union (C.P.S.U.), age, 38, 39, 42; city party organizations (gorkom), 76–77; education of members, 36–38, 43–44; elite membership (Central Committee), 40–54; general membership, 26, 27, 28–41; krai (kraikom), 76; oblast (obkom), 77, 80, 122–123, 124, 126–128; occupation of members, 32–34, 44–48; party structure and the economy, 121–130; primary party organizations, 125–156; problems of party specialists, 133–137; raion (raikom), 80–81, 122–124, 126–128; women members, 39

Congresses of the C.P.S.U.; *20th Congress*, 26, 28, 41, 57, 103; collective leadership, 106; Khrushchev report, 108–109; *21st Congress*, 103; *22nd Congress*, 50, 103; collective leadership, 106; Khrushchev's report, 115; *23rd Congress*, 25, 26, 36, 50, 103; Brezhnev's report, 109, 110; Kosygin's report, 115

Chief Political Administration, 61

co-optation, 40, 48–49, 66, 68–70

Council of Agricultural Technology, 63, 64, 65

Council of Ministers, 56; relation to functions of the Politburo, 60, 99, 100; relation to Party-State Control Commission, 131

Czechoslovakia, Soviet invasion of, 145, 149

Deutsch, Karl W., 4, 7; feedback theory of, 5–6; views on autonomy, 24

DeWitt, Nicholas, 59

elections, 91–92

feedback theory, 5–6

functionalism, 7–8; Mitchell's scheme of, 8–10; 139–140, 149–150

goal attainment, 22–23, 119–121

goal specification, 20–21

Gosplan, 64, 65, 77

Higher Party School (Moscow), 73, 76, 81, 89

Ilyichev, Leonid, 61, 62

integration, 13, 140; of parties, 15

Kapitanov, Ivan, 56

Kassof, Allen, 94

Khrushchev, Nikita S., and the anti-party crisis, 55; criticism of bureaucracy, 34, 107; conflict with Malenkov, 110–111; dismissal, 60; leadership of Central Committee, 60–63; and

managerial problems, 112–114; and party membership, 27, 33; and party organization, 30, 99–100, 105; report to 20th Congress, 104, 108–109; report to 22nd Congress, 115; view on party leadership, 106

Kirilenko, Andrei, 56

Komsomol, 32–42, 56, 63, 78; role as a youth organization, 94–96

Kosygin, Alexei, 115

Kozlov, Frol, 106

Kulakov, Fedor, 56

Linden, Carl, 101

Little Octobrists, 92

Machine Tractor Stations, 33, 34

Malenkov, Georgi, 99; conflict with Khrushchev, 110–111

Mensheviks, 141

Merton, Robert, 8

Meyer, Alfred, 4

Mikoyan, Anastas, 57

Mitchell, William, 8–10

movement-regime, definition of, 3

Neumann, Sigmund, 11, 12–13

New Economic Policy (N.E.P.), 146

nomenklatura, 132

Parsons, Talcott, 8

party, functions of, 11–12, 14–23 (Also see C.P.S.U.)

Party-State Control Commission, 130–133

Party Organs Department, 59

Podgornii, Nikolai, 57, 64; report at 22nd Congress, 109

Politburo, 56–56, 57–59; membership of, 101–102; role in decision-making, 100
political socialization, 15–17, 71–80, 96–97
Ponamarev, Boris, 56
propaganda, industrial, 84–88

recruitment, 17–20, 141
Rudakov, Alexander, 56

Secretariat, 54–55, 56–57
Selznick, Philip, 68, 69
Shelest, Pyotr, 57
Sorokin, P. A., 8
Stalin, Joseph V., 86; advisers of, 98; economic policy of, 112; primacy of bureaucracy under, 99; secret police and party under, 29–30

State Commission for New Technology, 77
State Committee on Land Resources, 63
State Committee on Radio and Television, 89–90
State Economic Commission, 76–77
Suslov, Mikhail, 56

Trade Union Congress, 56, 57
Tucker, Robert C., 3, 4; on mass movement-regimes, 3, 10

Union of Soviet Writers, 61
Ustinov, Dmitrii, 56

Weber, Max, 8

Young Pioneers, 92, 93, 94

Zhukov, Georgi, 55